VISION MACHINES

D1558864

Critical Studies in Latin American and Iberian Cultures

SERIES EDITORS:

James Dunkerley
John King

This major series – the first of its kind to appear in English – is designed to map the field of contemporary Latin American culture, which has enjoyed increasing popularity in Britain and the United States in recent years.

The series aims to broaden the scope of criticism of Latin American culture, which tends still to extol the virtues of a few established 'master' works and to examine cultural production within the context of twentieth-century history. These clear, accessible studies are aimed at those who wish to know more about some of the most important and influential cultural works and movements of our time.

Other Titles in the Series

VISION MACHINES

Cinema, Literature and Sexuality in Spain and Cuba, 1983–93

PAUL JULIAN SMITH

VERSO

London • New York

First published by Verso 1996
© Paul Julian Smith 1996
All rights reserved

Verso
UK: 6 Meard Street, London W1V 3HR
USA: 180 Varick Street, New York NY 10014–4606

Verso is the imprint of New Left Books

Plates 1–5, 8–11, 19 and 20 are from the collection of BFI Stills,
Posters and Designs. Plates 6 and 7 are from the collection of
Electric Pictures. Plates 12–18 appear by kind permission of Galería
La Máquina Española, Seville.

ISBN 1–85984–944–X
ISBN 1–85984–079–5 (pbk)

British Library Cataloguing in Publication Data
A catalogue record for this book is available from the British Library

Library of Congress Cataloging-in-Publication Data
Smith, Paul Julian.
Vision machines : cinema, literature, and sexuality in Spain and
Cuba, 1983–93 / Paul Julian Smith.
p.   cm. — (Critical studies in Latin American and Iberian culture)
Includes bibliographical references and index.
ISBN 1–85984–944–X (cl). — ISBN 1–85984–079–5 (pbk.)
1. Motion pictures—Social aspects—Spain. 2. Motion pictures—Social
aspects—Cuba. 3. Social problems in motion pictures. 4. Motion
pictures and literature—Spain. 5. Motion pictures and literature—Cuba.
I. Title. II. Series. PN1993.5.S7S53   1996
302.23′43′0946—dc20   95–43673 CIP

Typeset by Keystroke, Jacaranda Lodge, Wolverhampton.
Printed and bound in Great Britain by Biddles Ltd,
Guildford and King's Lynn

Barton to Agnon

CONTENTS

PREFACE

This book is not a cultural history of Spain and Cuba over a recent decade, but rather a series of case studies: analyses of particular texts in so far as they relate to visibility, sexuality and nationality. I make no claim to be exhaustive or representative of either country; indeed, in the case of Spain I focus to a large extent on the *autonomías* and in that of Cuba on work produced in exile. This book also marks a theoretical shift away from Anglo-American feminist film and queer theory to Continental work on technology, cinema and postmodernism, as exemplified by Paul Virilio, Serge Daney and Gianni Vattimo.

I would like to thank John King, the editor of this series, for his efficiency and encouragement; Philip Dodd, editor of *Sight and Sound*, for commissioning features from me on *Kika* and Cuban homosexualities, Jonathan Romney for commissioning a review of *La ardilla roja* and Millie Simpson, picture editor at *Sight and Sound*, for her help with stills; the staff at the British Film Institute Library and the Stills, Posters and Designs section; the Filmoteca Nacional and Biblioteca Nacional, Madrid; students and colleagues in the Faculty of Modern and Medieval Languages in the University of Cambridge; and the following individuals who kindly provided me with materials and/or bibliographic information: Juan Vicente Aliaga (without whom chapter 5 would not have been written), Emilie Bergmann, Benedict Carver, Catherine Davies, Jo Labanyi, Leah Middlebrook, Alberto Mira, Ryan Prout, David Vilaseca.

The chapters were read in various forms at the following places over the last two years. Chapter 1: Inaugural Lecture in the University of Cambridge; Harvard University (Annual Lecture in Memory of Professor Lida); Yale University; New York University; Johns Hopkins University, Baltimore, Md; Loyola College, Baltimore, Md; Princeton University; University of Virginia, Charlottesville, Va; Queen Mary and Westfield College, University of London; Instituto Cervantes, Leeds University; Guildhall University, London. Chapter 2: Spain Today, Dartmouth College, New Hampshire; Deutscher Hispanistentag, Bonn. Chapter 3: University of Kentucky at Lexington; Hispanisms and Homosexualities: New York University; Latin American Studies, Birmingham University. Chapter 5: New Directions in Modern Peninsular Studies, New York University; Jornadas sobre cultura lesbiana y gai, Universidad de Sevilla; Os Estudios gais e lesbianos en España, Universidade de Vigo.

Paul Julian Smith
London and Cambridge, June 1995

LIST OF ILLUSTRATIONS

INTRODUCTION:

Technology, Subjectivity, Solidarity

In Pedro Almodóvar's *Kika* (1993) video vamp Andrea (Victoria Abril) circles Madrid on her motorbike, taping everyday misfortunes (rapes, murders) with a camera inserted in her helmet. In the evening she broadcasts her videotapes on a TV programme called 'The Worst of the Day', sharing the scenes with a phantasmic, electronic audience. This reality show is sponsored by a dairy, Royal Milk.

In Reinaldo Arenas's autobiography *Antes que anochezca* (Before Night Falls, 1992), the author describes the aftermath of the Mariel exodus of 1980. Seizing his chance to leave, Arenas presents himself at a police station as a passive homosexual and is asked to walk in front of a psychologist in order to offer visual confirmation of his self-diagnosis. Having passed this test (and changed the name on his identity card), Arenas slips out of Cuba: 'I left as just another queen [*loca*], not as a writer.'[1]

In Pepe Espaliú's sculptures known as 'Carrying' (1992–3), sedan chairs made of iron are suspended above the spectator, piercing the gallery walls at odd angles. The chairs are hermetically sealed. Or again in 'El nido' (The Nest, 1993), metal crutches, painted prettily in pastels, are arranged in an unbroken circle, which excludes human participation even as it mutely points to the frailties of the body and to its dependence on mechanical prostheses.

These are three of the cultural phenomena I treat in this book. And while I do not seek to minimize the differences between

1

them (between Spanish and Cuban, between film, text and sculpture), still I believe they share certain characteristics. Those characteristics relate to what French historian of technology Paul Virilio (from whom I borrow the title of this book) has called the 'vision machine': a paradoxical condition in which it is the object which perceives the subject. More particularly, each of my opening examples illustrates a different aspect of what Virilio calls the 'evaporation of visual subjectivity'.[2] Thus Almodóvar foregrounds technology: the fusion or confusion of the real and the represented in the instantaneous moment of video. Arenas stresses discipline and subjectivity: a sense of self (here, of homosexual self) that is called into being by a trial of visibility in which deviants may be at once identified and expelled from the social body. Finally, Espaliú calls attention to solidarity and silence: an aesthetics of disappearance in which the artist (the subject) is represented only in his absence by resonant and enigmatic remainders which speak of disease and mortality.

An initial hypothesis, then, would be that visibility is constantly inflected by sexuality and nationality, that the three form a complex and productive constellation. The last decade has seen that constellation become a major theme in Spanish and Cuban cinema, literature and art.[3] This book attempts to address some of those texts in the light of both their historical context and recent theoretical accounts of the look, of sight and of representation.

The book is divided into three sections, each comprising two chapters. The first chapter in each section contrasts two artists or texts from the decade 1983 to 1993 and offers a general historical and theoretical account of the issue at hand: female sexuality in the wake of García Lorca; Cuban homosexualities; and AIDS in the Spanish state. The second gives a close reading of a single film produced in 1993: Almodóvar's *Kika*; Gutiérrez Alea's *Fresa y chocolate* (Strawberry and Chocolate); Julio Medem's *La ardilla roja* (The Red Squirrel). Chapter 1 explores the woman's look in Almodóvar's *Entre tinieblas* (Dark Habits, 1983) with reference to Teresa de Lauretis's work on film and the visible. It argues that Almodóvar lesbianizes the matriarchal household derived from García Lorca's *La casa de Bernarda Alba* (The House of Bernarda Alba) and contrasts Mario Camus's 1987 film version of that play (exemplary of state-sponsored filmmaking of the period) with Almodóvar's more deviant techniques. Chapter 2 draws on Paul

2

Virilio's *The Vision Machine* to explore the relations between cinema and video in *Kika*, arguing that the film fuses or confuses presentation and representation, shifting from the dialectical duration of celluloid to the paradoxical instant of electronic real time. It also suggests how the vision machine can be gendered by referring to the work on visual technologies by US feminists de Lauretis and Donna Haraway.

Chapter 3 examines the reception in Europe and North America of cinematographer Néstor Almendros's documentary on gays in Cuba *Mauvaise conduite* (Improper Conduct, 1984), tracing the trial of visibility to which effeminate men were exposed and arguing that the oppression of homosexuals was not fortuitous, but rather structurally determined by the centrality of the labour theory of value to Marxist theory. Picking up on the paradoxes of Almendros's quest for 'natural light' in his auto-biography *Man with a Camera*,[4] it compares Almendros's reticence (about both homosexuality and AIDS) with the flamboyance of exile novelist Reinaldo Arenas, whose autobiography *Antes que anochezca* offers a graphic depiction of queer Cuba. Chapter 4 examines Oscar-nominated *Fresa y chocolate*, the first Cuban film to focus on a gay theme, reading it in the light of director Gutiérrez Alea's essay on 'the dialectic of the spectator' and French film critic Serge Daney's analysis of vision and visuals.

Chapter 5 attempts an account of representations of AIDS in Spain, the country which currently suffers the highest rate of increase in HIV transmission in Europe. An invisible epidemic, characterized by denial and distrust, AIDS has until recently received as little response from artists and intellectuals as from politicians and health-care professionals. Drawing on Anglo-American debates on representing AIDS (Simon Watney, Cindy Patton) and attempting to reread them in a Spanish context, the chapter focuses on the first major response by Spanish scholars and artists to AIDS, *De amor y rabia* (Of Love and Rage),[5] and on the major figure in any medium to address the epidemic in his aesthetic practice, conceptual artist and videomaker Pepe Espaliú. The final chapter takes postmodernist philosopher Gianni Vattimo as a guide to the visual labyrinths of Basque filmmaker Julio Medem's *La ardilla roja*, suggesting that this ludic and oneiric thriller at once challenges the stereotypes of female and ethnic invisibility and repeats those stereotypes in radically 'weakened' and distorted form. Medem's playful approach to the supposed dark continents of femininity and ethnicity opens up a chance for a new conception of heterosexuality and a new understanding of the regional and dialectal.

Clearly my chosen field is a vast one, and I claim neither that my survey is exhaustive nor that my chosen texts are representative. However, it is possible at this initial stage to sketch some of the theoretical problems involved in such a project. Martin Jay has given an excellent account of the 'denigration of vision' in Foucault and others, examining the 'anti-visual discourse' and 'interrogation of sight' in twentieth-century French thought.[6] Jay finds in Foucault a number of insights which recur, in slightly different form, in the theorists I cite and to which Jay does not refer. These points include: the mortal terror of the penetrating, medical gaze which 'opens up to the light of day the black coffer of the body' (p. 182); the relation between the hostility to visual primacy and the critique of humanism (p. 186); the transcendental (humanist) subject as a function, not a precondition, of ocular-centrism (p. 190); 'the dream of a transparent society, visible and legible in each of its parts, the dream of there no longer existing any zones of darkness', which is the ambition of Revolutionary terror (p. 192); and finally the twin complementary and opposed themes of surveillance of sexuality, 'inscribed in [institutional] architecture', and the flagrancy of the sexual 'pervert', whose deviance was 'written immodestly on his face and body because it was a secret that always gave itself away' (p. 193).

Paul Virilio extends and literalizes Foucault's critique of Enlightenment rationality and the mortal, disciplinary gaze. In *War and Cinema* (first published in French in 1984),[7] Virilio traces a 'logistics of perception' in which twentieth-century visualizing technology is coextensive with death. From aerial photography to video surveillance, eyeshot coincides with gunshot, in a quest for 'the ideal alignment of the look' (p. 2) in which, finally, 'what is perceived is already lost' (p. 4). Recent 'stealth' weapons invest in concealment, an 'aesthetics of disappearance' which is the dark and necessary shadow of 'a technicians' version of an all-seeing Divinity, ever ruling out accident and surprise, . . . a general system of illumination that will allow everything to be seen and known, at every moment and in every place' (p. 4). As later in *The Vision Machine* (first published in 1988), man's 'exaggerated love of light', his 'illuminating [of] himself [as] the subject of positive knowledge' brings 'tragedy' (pp. 35, 36); and the 'multiplying

4

proofs of reality' produced by photography serve merely to 'exhaust' the real (p. 22).

Virilio's technological pessimism seems so pervasive that it comes as a surprise to find him marshalling his theories to address a specific political crisis. But in an article on the then current election of Silvio Berlusconi to the office of Italian prime minister, Virilio attacks 'cathodic democracy', arguing that the old choice between left and right has given way to an alternation of 'the political' and 'the media' in which the audiovisual preempts any political programme, displacing the parliamentary project as a whole.[8] It is a position also taken by the best-known theorist of postmodernism in Spain, Italian philosopher Gianni Vattimo. The 'transparent society'[9] of Vattimo is parallel to Foucault's and Virilio's Enlightenment nightmare: it is a mediatized society in which there is 'no authentic political emancipation . . . but the logic of information economy [which] requires continuous expansion of itself' (p. 79). When 'event' and 'news' are one and the same (p. 89), then a 'transcendental subject' takes up its position at the centre, lord of all it surveys. However, just as Virilio's critique of all-pervasive visualizing technology does not preclude political intervention, so Vattimo's diagnosis of transparency does not imply fatalism. Rather the 'erosion of the reality principle' effected by the 'explosion of visions of the world' (p. 79) leads to opacity and 'noise'. And if it is not possible to separate civil society from the media, still the former is not reducible to the latter (p. 91). History may (as in Virilio) have been reduced to 'simultaneity . . . real time' (p. 96), but still tradition is lived as visible traces in our bodies. In chapter 6 I argue that such is Julio Medem's account of images of femininity and Basqueness, which are evacuated, distorted but preserved in subtly weakened form in *La ardilla roja*.

Visibility and transparency also come under theoretical suspicion in the critique of representation which is familiar from such diverse sources as Marxism and structuralism. In my discussion of Cuban homosexualities in the central chapters of this book, I argue for a sensitivity to context in the use of such powerful conceptual tools. Thus while Althusser and Barthes used sophisticated versions of ideology or mythology to render visible the naturalized political investments in cultural products of powerful state apparatuses, those same techniques were later used to disqualify the testimony of the survivors of state terror in Cuba.

Documentary and autobiography, the genres I treat here, thus pose particular problems for cultural critics who reject 'the straight line from the real to the visible' often held to be typical of bourgeois realist fiction and classical Hollywood cinema, but wish to pay proper respect to the 'little' (but cumulative) narratives of personal witnesses. If we cannot simply accept that 'claim to the real'[10] to which such genres aspire, still we cannot rule out the possibility of reference and truth. Here I draw on an ethical model, ultimately derived from Levinas, of 'the truth of the face': respect for the other in its very separation from the self, in its persistence in time and mortality. It is an ethics of the body also suggested by the later work of French gay critic Serge Daney, veteran of the *Cahiers du Cinéma* 'politics of representation', which was once one of the strongest supporters of the Cuban cinematic and political experiment.

Daney laments the death or decline of cinema in the shift 'from vision to visuals'; and he tends to focus, perversely, on a single, simple detail of a film (a window or a shoe). It is an attention to detail also characteristic of a French theorist notorious for his supposed apoliticism and irresponsibility, Jean Baudrillard. Moving out of Marx's critique of capital, Baudrillard replaces production by simulation and commodities by simulacra: social practice is now held to be a circulation of copies which have no originals, of images deprived of use value.[11] In his particular version of the vision machine, Baudrillard cites (like Foucault and Virilio) medicine and the military: the simulation of disease still produces observable symptoms; army personnel who act crazy are treated as crazy (p. 168). The old 'wager on representation' is dead, the 'dialectical capacity of representations as a visible and intelligible mediation of the real' (p. 170) confounded by the loss of a supreme being (God, man) to guarantee symbolic exchange. The process of simulation cannot be isolated, nor the 'mourning for the real' completed (pp. 178, 181). When 'things have found a way to elude the dialectic of meaning', abolishing the distinction between illusion and appearance (p. 185), then the role of art, as of the event, is simply to 'stage its own mode of disappearance' (pp. 188, 192). The contemporary scene is like Pompeii: a suspended catastrophe highlighting the 'transparency of the smallest detail' (p. 197), and a mute witness to a generalized 'drive to spectacle' (p. 202).

Yet, as I argue in chapter 5, Baudrillard's 'fatal strategy' (with its stress on paradox, irony and disappearance) coincides with the response of many Spanish artists and intellectuals to AIDS. And, like Espaliú's mute, ironic circle of crutches, Baudrillard's 'haemorrhaging of value' need not inevitably preclude a certain solidarity in the face of catastrophe, but rather suggests, in its Spanish reception at least, a paradoxical but finally ethical response to human mortality and the remainder of the body.

Although Vattimo makes occasional reference to 'blacks, women, and gays' as exemplary nontranscendental subjects, he and the other theorists cited above are typical of Continental theory in paying little or no attention to questions of gender and sexuality which are so familiar to Anglo-Americans.[12] And while I have chosen in this book not to go over once more the psychoanalytic 'gaze theory' which has been so fruitful and influential in English-language film studies, I both tease out the implications of the vision machine for women and gay men, and appeal to the gendering of technology in two feminist scholars, de Lauretis and Haraway. De Lauretis reminds us that the problem of 'spectatorship . . . central to the feminist critique of representation' remains a problem and cannot simply be solved by the appeal to empirical, lesbian women's reappropriation of dominant texts.[13] Rather she stresses the insistence of gender and the 'residue' of sexual difference (p. 169), even as it is subjectively absorbed by the lesbian spectator who finds herself addressed by visual technology. Donna Haraway goes further,[14] citing, like Virilio, a 'border war between organism and machine' (p. 150), provoked, again as in Virilio, by the 'ubiquity and invisibility of cyborgs . . . machines made of sunshine' (p. 153). The cyborg 'simulates politics' (p. 163). But, as in Baudrillard, simulation cannot be isolated from the real: reproductive technologies render 'women's bodies . . . newly permeable to both "visualization" and "intervention"', revealing the 'predatory nature of photographic consciousness' (p. 169). The effects of technology are thus by no means sexually indifferent and must have varied implications for both the subjectivity and the solidarity of women and gay men.

In a preface to the Spanish translation, *La sociedad transparente*, Vattimo assumes the risk of presenting Spain as a model of post-modernism, the latter understood as a 'chance of emancipation that is neither a Hegelian-Marxist dialectical reappropriation nor a neo-Catholic return to the sacred, to community, to the family'

(p. 67). It is surely ironic that, revising Benjamin, Vattimo should cite Madrid as the 'capital of the twentieth century'; for one aspect of that 'lighter social rationality' (p. 71) praised by Vattimo is the fragmentation of the Spanish state, which now has no single centre. Vattimo's is a dangerous appeal to a shared 'Latin accent' which has also been taken up by other commentators. Teresa Vilarós cites Vattimo's statement when she proposes post-Francoism as the place of the feather (*pluma*): volatility, chaotic excess and a generalized camp or gay male sensibility.[15] Cultural historian and film scholar Agustín Sánchez Vidal also sees this period as a 'lightening' of historical and metaphysical loads, claiming that Spaniards 'dismounted' from History (with a capital letter), rediscovering the little pleasures and narratives of everyday life.[16] This is not the place for a cultural history of Spain (or of Cuba and its diaspora) in the 1980s. But, having sketched the theoretical debate, it may be useful to give a brief account of some cultural conditions affecting the texts I examine and to which I refer intermittently throughout the book.

Nineteen eighty-three saw a briefly optimistic moment in the Spanish art world. In the visual arts the second meeting of the state-sponsored ARCO, the international Festival of Contemporary Art, proved a massive success: Madrid was in the grip of 'art fever'.[17] State scholarships and grants enabled young artists such as Pepe Espaliú to break the traditional isolation and increasingly to work abroad:[18] in a recent exhibition as part of a Spanish Arts Festival in London, aptly named *Mudanzas* ('changes' or 'moves'), only one of the six young artists was permanently based in Spain.[19] But at the same time that it sponsored nomadism, the state promoted contemporary and often experimental art as an image of its own modernization as a constitutional monarchy: the massive new Madrid museum was named for and sponsored by Queen Sofía; a full-page portrait of the royal couple preceded the catalogue to the Spanish art exhibition prominent at Expo 1992 in Seville.[20]

In cinema, the celebrated Miró law of 1983 (devised by the new Socialist head of film production) introduced a new and more favourable 'screen quota', effectively forcing reluctant domestic distributors to take Spanish films, while offering filmmakers 50 per cent subsidies set against the grosses of subsequent productions.[21] Struggling young directors such as Almodóvar (who had released *Entre tinieblas* in 1983) were able to convert themselves into producers, paid by the government to do so. However lavishly promoted in New York, Paris and London, still Spanish producers failed to sell their films abroad.[22] Nor did their films retain market share at home. Why was this the case? A glance at the glossy programme for the Third Festival of Films from Spain held in New York in 1987 provides some hints. Almodóvar's sleekest melo-drama *Matador* (1985) stands out at once; more typical, however, are Vicente Aranda's adaptation of the classic novel *Tiempo de silencio* (Time of Silence, 1986) and Pilar Miró's reworking of Goethe's *Werther* (1986). Such elegantly costumed and tastefully photographed pieces were typical of the 'quality' filmmaking promoted by the subsidy system (Mario Camus's *Bernarda Alba* was another). It was a policy that laid itself open to charges of patronage and cultural elitism.[23] At least one historian of Spanish film (José Enrique Monterde) sees a continuous conflict or 'paradox' between the industry's dependence on state protectionism and its desire for artistic freedom from the Franco period to the 1990s.[24] Moreover, in the words of Miró's successor, Fernando Méndez-Leite, state subsidy was not a 'piece of chewing gum' that could be stretched out for ever; nor could it compete with the vertical integration of Hollywood and the increasing homogeniza-tion and globalization of media markets.[25] The commercial and artistic decline of Spanish cinema (with exceptions such as Almodóvar) seemed inevitable. And if artists tended towards fruit-ful migration outside of the Spanish state, filmmakers, less mobile, were beset by quarrels between the autonomous regions.[26]

By the 1980s Cuban cinema was also in something of a crisis, in spite of the replacement of veteran Alfredo Guevara by Julio García Espinosa as head of cinema at the Ministry of Culture[27] and the emergence of younger directors such as Juan Carlos Tabío, later to share the directing credit for *Fresa y chocolate* with Gutiérrez Alea. While Michael Chanan, writing mid decade, was bullish about the future of the 'new ways of seeing' initiated by directors who had produced their best work for the monopoly film institute (ICAIC) shortly after the Revolution of 1959,[28] later commentators were not so sanguine. Paulo Antonio Paranagua notes that from the 1970s onwards Cuban filmmakers 'turned back to the past', neglecting what Jesús Díaz has called 'the challenges of contemporaneity' that had been addressed in such innovatory style by such films of the 1960s as Gutiérrez Alea's *Memorias de subdesarrollo* (Memories of Underdevelopment).[29]

Most recently Timothy Barnard has traced the history of what he calls the 'past-present tense' in Cuban film.[30] Where filmmakers Julio García Espinosa and Tomás Gutiérrez Alea had proposed a Utopian merging of life and art in which art 'will disappear into everything', creating 'an organic integration of form and content' (Barnard, p. 233), the practice was the dominance of the historical genre, which became 'a decadent, insipid shadow of its former self' in films such as Solás's lengthy literary adaptation *Cecilia* (1982) and Enrique Pineda Barnet's insubstantial period piece *La bella del Alhambra* (The Belle of the Alhambra, 1989). As in the very different circumstances of Spain, then, state sponsorship, artistic dependency on a single political party, financial crisis and corruption combined to produce a sometimes pedestrian film industry enlivened by occasional innovations, in subject matter if not in style, such as Gutiérrez Alea's *Fresa y chocolate*. Barnard asks of Cuban period pieces: 'Are these films formal representations of an ideology which has set about to intervene in history in order to create a need for the present?' (p. 240). It is a question eerily relevant to Spain also, where a Socialist government backed 'quality' projects, such as *Bernarda Alba*, that served to remind reluctant domestic audiences both of the splendour of their cultural heritage and of the brutality of a repressive past from which the democratic, left-leaning present had redeemed them.

In Cuba, 1983 saw the Fourth International Festival of New Latin American Cinema (a successful marketplace) and the following year the Twelfth Meeting of Heads of Film Production in the Socialist Countries.[31] Nineteen eighty-four was also the twenty-fifth anniversary of the Revolution, marked by the long-running journal *Cine Cubano* with a 'Letter to Fidel' from the directors of ICAIC, saluting the leader as the 'founder of Cuban cinematography'.[32] New schemes were launched to promote domestic film production, such as the founding of the International School of Film and Television based at San Antonio de los Baños under the auspices of Gabriel García Márquez[33] and the division of ICAIC into three sections under the tutelage of prestigious directors Gutiérrez Alea, Solás and Manuel Pérez (King, p. 165). In spite of an increase in contemporary subjects, still Cuban cinema clung to the 'past-present tense' and recycled recent history: *Cine Cubano* went on celebrating the successive anniversaries of the revolutionary calendar as the 'Socialist countries' disappeared and Cuba was plunged into economic crisis.

It would be foolish to call too much attention to the parallels between Spanish and Cuban cultural histories in the 1980s. However, there is a dense 'traffic' (Serge Daney's term) of movement in both directions between the two countries, as there is between Hispanic texts and non-Hispanic theory: Mario Camus is received in Havana[34] and Telemadrid coproduces *Fresa y chocolate*; Pepe Espaliú attends Lacan's seminar in Paris and French company Ciby 2000 coproduces *Kika*. Andrea's reality show, Arenas's trial of visibility, Espaliú's sedan chairs and crutches, each is indelibly marked by the time and place in which they were forged. But that place is also displaced (as regionalism, internationalism and exile), just as sexuality is splintered (into lesbian, gay and straight). And the visualizing technology which is my main theme is at once theoretical and historical: after reading Virilio's account of Enlightenment illumination we can never look in quite the same way at such apparently innocent innovations as street lighting. Seeking out and inadvertently intensifying shadowy opacities and deviations, technology thus intersects with subjectivity and solidarity in complex and productive ways.

In a recent interview Almodóvar tells the story of how he sought a visual hook, a resonant image to place above the bed of a character in the film he was currently shooting.[35] With the death or decline of religion he can no longer use a Catholic icon; he chooses rather to place a gold-framed map of Spain in this prominent position, symbolizing 'the map (and the knowledge) [he] was denied as a child', subjected as he was to the brutality and ignorance of a National-Catholic education. The map that precedes or displaces the territory is a motif of both Vattimo and Baudrillard;[36] it is also a glowing and resonant icon of the lush visuals of Almodóvar's cinema, one which is to be contrasted, as we shall see, with the more modest visual ambitions of Socialist cultural policy.

NOTES

1   Reinaldo Arenas, *Antes que anochezca* (Barcelona: Tusquets, 1992), p. 302.

2   Paul Virilio, *The Vision Machine* (London: BFI, 1994), p. 47.

3   As some 10 per cent of Cubans now live off the island I use the term in the broad sense to include the diaspora work of those such as Arenas and Almendros; for the extended sense of Cuban cinema see Ana M. López,

'Cuban Cinema in Exile: The "Other" Island', *Jump Cut*, no. 38 (1993), pp. 51–9.

4   Almendros, often cited as the world's greatest cinematographer, goes unmentioned in International Federation of Film Archives (FIAF), *International Directory of Cinematographers, Set and Costume Designers in Film: Volume 12: Cuba (From the Beginnings to 1990)*, ed. Alfred Krautz, coord. Lourdes Castro Ramos (Munich, London, New York, Paris: K. G. Saur, 1992), perhaps because the directory excludes documentaries such as those Almendros shot in the Cuba of the 1960s.

5   Juan Vicente Aliaga and José Miguel G. Cortés, eds, *De amor y rabia* (Valencia: Universidad Politécnica de Valencia, 1993).

6   Martin Jay, 'In the Empire of the Gaze: Foucault and the Denigration of Vision in Twentieth-Century French Thought', in David Couzens Hoy, ed., *Foucault: A Critical Reader* (Oxford: Blackwell, 1986), pp. 175–204.

7   Paul Virilio, *War and Cinema* (London: Verso, 1989).

8   Paul Virilio, 'La vanguardia del olvido', *El País* (13 May 1994), pp. 13, 14.

9   I cite the Spanish translation by Teresa Oñate, *La sociedad transparente* (Barcelona: Paidós, 1992).

10 Brian Winston, *Claiming the Real: The Documentary Film Revisited* (London: BFI, 1995).

11 Jean Baudrillard, *Selected Writings*, ed. Mark Poster (Cambridge: Polity, 1988).

12 De Lauretis notes that 'the notion of gender is untranslatable in any Romance language'. Teresa de Lauretis, *Technologies of Gender: Essays on Theory, Film, and Fiction* (London: Macmillan, 1987), p. 4. This has not, of course, prevented some scholars in Spain, Italy or France from addressing sexual difference in film. For another, historical account of the relation between reproductive technology and gender, with particular reference to 'bachelor machines', see Peter Wollen, 'Modern Times: Cinema/Americanism/The Robot', in *Raiding the Icebox: Reflections on Twentieth-Century Culture* (London: Verso, 1993), pp. 35–71.

13 Teresa de Lauretis, 'Sexual Indifference and Lesbian Representation', *Theater Journal* 40 (1988), pp. 155–77.

14 Donna J. Haraway, *Simians, Cyborgs, and Women* (London: Free Association, 1991).

15 Teresa Vilarós, 'Revuelo de plumas en la España de la transición', *Revista Cultural de Crítica* 8 (May 1994), pp. 20–5.

16 Augustín Sánchez Vidal, *Sol y sombra* (Barcelona: Planeta, 1990).

17 John Hooper, *The Spaniards* (London: Penguin, 1987), p. 156.

18 Teresa Blanch, '1982–92: Spain at the Beginning of a Well Defined Intersection', in *Pasajes: Spanish Art Today* (Seville: Electa, 1992), pp. 23–32. This is the catalogue for the exhibition of contemporary art in the Spanish Pavilion at the Expo; Pepe Espaliú was amongst the artists

selected. The catalogue notes say that '[his] ideas . . . define those of Spanish artists in the second half of the eighties' (p. 74).

19   *Mudanzas* (Whitechapel Gallery, 25 February–24 April 1994). The artists were Victoria Civera, Susy Gómez, Paloma Pelaez, Joan Rom, Juan Uslé and Eulàlia Valldosa. Most are based in New York.

20   See *Pasajes*, note 18 above.

21   John Hopewell, *Out of the Past: Spanish Cinema After Franco* (London: BFI, 1986), p. 226.

22   John Hopewell, 'Look through Spanish Eyes', *Moving Pictures* (18 November 1993), p. 12.

23   *Out of the Past*, p. 231; John Hooper, *The New Spaniards* (London: Penguin, 1995), p. 339. This updated volume provides the most accessible guide to current cultural policy in Spain.

24   José Enrique Monterde, *Veinte años de cine español: un cine bajo la paradoja* (Barcelona: Paidós, 1993), p. 201.

25   John Hopewell, *El cine español después de Franco* (Madrid: El Arquero, 1989), p. 463.

26   See most recently Rupert Widdicombe, 'Catalan Quota Sparks Backlash', *Screen International* (19 November 1993), p. 4; and Rocío García, 'Roca y Carmen Alborch acuerdan la paz en el conflicto sobre el cine catalán', *El País* (9 February 1994).

27   John King, *Magical Reels: A History of Cinema in Latin America* (London: Verso, 1990), p. 161.

28   Michael Chanan, *The Cuban Image* (London: BFI, 1985), p. 297.

29   Paulo Antonio Paranagua, ed., *Le Cinéma cubain* (Paris: Centre Pompidou, 1990).

30   Timothy Barnard, 'Death Is Not True', in John King, Ana M. López and Manuel Alvarado, eds, *Mediating Two Worlds: Cinematic Encounters in The Americas* (London: BFI, 1993), pp. 230–41.

31   *Cine Cubano* 105 (1983) and 109 (1984).

32   *Cine Cubano* 109 (1984), p. 1.

33   For an account of Castro's inaugural visit to the school see *Cine Cubano* 117 (1987), p. 117.

34   *Cine Cubano* 111 (1985). Other Spanish directors such as Saura and Bardem also made visits during this period. Perhaps the most intriguing example of cross-cultural traffic is Eneko Olasagasti and Carlos Zabala's *Maité* (1995), a Basque–Cuban coproduction.

35   Pedro Almodóvar, 'The Pain in Spain', *Time Out* (London, 10–17 May 1995), p. 74.

36   *La sociedad transparente*, p. 81; *Selected Writings*, p. 166.

PART I

Almodóvar's Women

1

GARCÍA LORCA/ALMODÓVAR:

Gender, Nationality and the Limits of the Visible

1. THE STANDARD OF VISION

I have described that first meeting with Federico García Lorca before. It sounds, now, too romantic to be true; but it was true in 1919. . . . That evening there had been a concert at the Arts Club, the Círculo de Bellas Artes. Falla, the composer, was there in the audience. Actually it was he who had brought me; and afterwards it seemed that 'of course' we were to go to someone's garden in the oldest and most picturesque part of Granada, the Albaicín. It was already midnight, but we dawdled in the main street, eating prickly pears which someone had bought off a barrow; and then were led up the steep, cobbled streets to a plain door in a high wall. It opened into a large dark garden full of the sound of running water. . . . Then we were hushed and a rather shy youth recited. He did not declaim, but spoke in a soft, warm, eager voice: *la obscura, cálida, turbia inolvidable voz de Federico García Lorca*, Gerardo Diego said long afterwards. 'Who is it?' 'Federico García Lorca. You must meet him.' The evening ended after 4 a.m., with the poet and myself, arm in arm, helping one another down the steep streets of the Albaicín, to the main street and the bottom of the Alhambra Hill. *¡Noche, que noche nochera!*

This account of a meeting between two remarkable men is by J.B. Trend, one of the most distinguished British Hispanists of his time.[1] Trend was one of the first scholars from outside Spain to

17

hear Lorca speak, the first to witness a talent as yet unrecognized elsewhere. Seventy years after that meeting, I begin this first chapter with a passage by Trend not only because of the belle lettrist lyricism of its style, so typical of its period, but because it poses general questions which remain vital today and which will be developed throughout this book. These questions are those of gender, nationality and sexuality. And what interests me (what disturbs and delights me) in this passage is the way in which these topics are at once asserted and denied by Trend. Thus the seductive picture of Granada he paints is implicitly gendered as feminine, with its lush liquidity and warm sensuality. Yet women are conspicuously absent from this locus amoenus, the enclosed garden of a cultural performance restricted to male actors. Then, Spain is depicted as the place of the cultural Other, of a picturesque exoticism Trend compares to distant Araby. Yet this orientalist fantasy is punctured by Trend himself, when he notes that compared to the recent horrors of war in northern Europe, life in Spain is perfectly normal, civilization itself. Finally, the passage describes a scene of (metaphorical) seduction, an 'impossibly romantic' night which ends with the poet and scholar stumbling arm in arm down the Albaicín at four o'clock in the morning. Yet Trend is anxious to reassure us that Lorca was not a sexual being, claiming, 'The Lorca I knew was not oversexed; on the contrary.' Ultimately, Trend's ambivalence derives from an unacknowledged shift between desire and identification: on the one hand, he is attracted to a Spain which remains exotic, different; on the other, he identifies with a Spain which embodies the essence of a common humanity, a universal poetic culture.

Gender, nationality, sexuality: the three are intertwined, indeed inextricable, not only in foreign depictions of Spain (and Spanish America) as places of blood and passion, of implicitly presocial and unconscious drives, but also in Hispanic accounts of the nation as a motherland which must be defended from internal or external aggression. But what of texts which depict only women? What of texts in which the mother is not an object charged with symbolic value but a subject invested with material power? I examine two such texts here, by Spain's greatest twentieth-century dramatist and best-known contemporary filmmaker: García Lorca's *La casa de Bernarda Alba* (The House of Bernarda Alba, 1936) and Pedro Almodóvar's *Entre tinieblas* (Dark Habits, 1983). In both, women actors (absent from Trend's homosocial Granada) are defiantly visible. I ask three questions of these texts. First, how do they represent the relations between the women on stage (on screen) and the men outside the diegetic space? Second, how do the all-female communities they depict serve as allegories of the nation at a particular historical moment? Third, how do the texts represent relations between women, particularly in respect to identification and desire? At this point in my argument I draw on recent essays by feminist and film theorist Teresa de Lauretis on 'sexual indifference'.[2] De Lauretis argues (after Irigaray and others) that relations 'between' the sexes are in fact founded on an exclusion of the feminine which renders relations between women invisible, inconceivable:

> The difficulty in defining an autonomous form of female sexuality and desire in the wake of a cultural tradition . . . still grounded in sexual (in)difference, is not to be overlooked or wilfully bypassed. It is perhaps even greater than the difficulty in devising strategies of representation which will, in turn, alter the standard of vision, the frame of reference of visibility, of what can be seen. ('Sexual Indifference', pp. 170–1)

It may be misguided or inappropriate to seek the answers to such questions in texts authored by men. I shall argue, however, that both works, in very different ways, gesture towards an autonomous form of female sexuality and desire; and that both do so not by presenting positive images of women, but by attempting strategies of representation which displace, momentarily at least, conventional ways of seeing. By placing the pleasure of the woman's look at the centre of their theatre and cinema, García Lorca and Almodóvar may alter the standard of vision, of what can be seen.

One perhaps disturbing aspect of de Lauretis's critique of that standard is her suggestion that the interests of lesbian women may not always be identical with those of heterosexual feminists, in so far as the latter view gender and sexual difference as identical terms ('Sexual Indifference', p. 155). I argue in this chapter, following de Lauretis, that it is the 'female, reproductive body that paradoxically guarantees the eros between men' (p. 157); and that there is a 'double movement', manifest but repressed in García Lorca and Almodóvar, 'whereby men project their own sexuality on to women only to reabsorb it themselves in the guise of a feminine character' (p. 158). It does not follow, however, that sexual similarity (say, lesbianism) can simply displace sexual (in)difference in the effort to 'dislodge the erotic from the discourse on gender' (p. 159). Rather it is the case that efforts to escape gender are complex and contradictory; and the overtly same-sex drama which conserves traditional forms may prove less challenging to spectatorial norms than narratives which insist, perversely, on the residue of gender and thus render visible the hidden preconceptions of commercial cinema through a spectacle of the female body in or as excess.

Both *Bernarda Alba* and *Entre tinieblas* take place within the hermetically enclosed spaces of female communities: in *Bernarda Alba* the provincial house in which a tyrannical mother holds sway over her daughters; in *Entre tinieblas* the Madrid convent in which a ruthless and capricious Mother Superior oversees her nuns. Both can be read as allegories of Spain: the first warns, on the eve of the Civil War, of the perils of a repressive regime; the second testifies somewhat ambiguously to a libertarian moment in Spanish history shortly after the definitive consolidation of democracy. Finally, both focus on erotic rivalry amongst women: in the first, five sisters compete for a man who never appears on stage; in the second, five nuns compete for the affections of a glamorous female intruder. These texts challenge sexual indifference not at the level of content, but at that of the theatrical or cinematic apparatus. The distinction is thrown into relief by Mario Camus's film adaptation of *Bernarda Alba*, made in 1987. Camus's somewhat anaemic style of filmmaking (typical of cinema under the Socialists) contrasts with the performative excess characteristic of both García Lorca and Almodóvar.[3] Ironically, *Entre tinieblas*, written by Almodóvar for the screen, is far more theatrical, more dramatic, than Camus's naturalistic version of Lorca's original.[4]

My argument will thus be historical as well as theoretical. The twin matriarchs of Lorca and Almodóvar are to be read within a tradition of Spanish misogyny which is particularly marked in cinema under and after Franco. For mothers and daughters, visibility is bought only at the cost of annihilation by the men who have created them. Through the twin themes of incest and matricide male artists project the power and horror of Fascism on to an omnipotent matriarch who must then be destroyed. As we shall see, by invoking yet eluding this double gesture (of projection and extermination) Almodóvar signals his ambivalent engagement with the cultural tradition in which he works and on which he is dependent.

2. *BERNARDA ALBA*:
SEXUAL INDIFFERENCE

The subtitle of *Bernarda Alba* is 'Drama of women in the villages of Spain'.[5] García Lorca's tragedy of dictatorship and oppression is thus qualified from the very beginning by reference to the gender and nationality of the actors who perform it. And the play offers uncompromising comments on the inevitable subservience of women to men. In Act 1 Bernarda claims it is woman's lot to mourn men, thus justifying the incarceration of her daughters. And she offers an unambiguous division of labour: 'Needle and thread for females; whips and mules for males' (p. 15). In Act 3 La Poncia (the housekeeper and voice of moderation) claims that 'a man is a man' and that the sisters are frustrated simply because they are 'women without men' (pp. 80–1). Yet this division of power attributed to men and women is redistributed within the play itself amongst women. Now the father is dead, it is Bernarda who rules a female household, and she does not hesitate to use a whip on her rebellious daughters. In this tragedy of sexual indifference, Bernarda's walking stick is the phallus which enforces the male order of dominance and subordination. It is no accident that in some productions Bernarda has been played by a male actor.

Yet this internalization of gender roles is by no means natural or eternal. Rather it is inscribed within a complex web of class and nationality. Bernarda's dictum on needles and whips is followed by the qualifier: 'This is the lot of people with means' (p. 15). And if it is indeed 'the greatest punishment to have been born a woman', then that punishment is felt with peculiar intensity by women from the landowning class. In the first scene, Bernarda dismisses the poor as 'animals . . . made from a different substance' to her family (p. 9). The line not only establishes the cruelty of her character; it also suggests that this drama will engage with social questions other than gender.

In his monumental biography of García Lorca, Ian Gibson places the composition of this his last play within the social and political context of Spain on the eve of the Civil War.[6] Quoting the dramatist's well-known claim that the play was not literature, but 'pure theatre', not poetry but 'pure realism', Gibson cites real-life prototypes for the play's characters in the aptly named village of Asquerosa (literally, 'disgusting') in the province of Granada

(pp. 435–6). According to Gibson, aspects of life in Asquerosa are reproduced without change in the play: the introspective character of the village; the excessively long periods of mourning commonly observed; the gossipy voyeurism and love of sexual scandal (p. 437). However, Gibson also reads the play as an allegory of despotism in a Spain menaced by the possibility of a right-wing coup.[7] Bernarda's hypocrisy, Catholicism and tyranny thus represent political authoritarianism; youngest daughter Adela's struggle against her mother a revolutionary commitment (p. 438). In an interview given to the liberal newspaper *El Sol* in the same month he completed *Bernarda Alba*, García Lorca speaks out against the doctrine of art for art's sake and in favour of a politically engaged theatre. And, interestingly, he links this to a rereading of Spanish history and nationality: the fall of Granada in 1492 (which marked the end of Muslim rule over Spanish territory) was a 'disaster', the loss of a civilization far superior to that of the Christian bourgeoisie who succeeded it. And if he (García Lorca) is a Spaniard through and through, he is also a complete cosmopolitan, closer to a good Chinaman (he claims) than to a bad Spaniard (p. 439).

García Lorca wrote that *Bernarda Alba* should be read as a 'photographic documentary'. While this phrase has been much debated by critics, it seems clear that there is a conflict in the play between a naturalistic attempt to depict the conditions of women in the provinces and an allegorical impulse to provide a metaphor for the Spanish political condition. And this conflict is felt nowhere more keenly than in the depiction of relations between women. I have already suggested that the play is 'sexually indifferent'; that is, that it uses female protagonists to enact a male drama of phallic dominance and submission. Moreover, as the last of García Lorca's rural tragedies, *Bernarda Alba* is a substitute for a work the dramatist planned but did not write which was to be called either *The Daughters of Lot* or *The Fall of Sodom*. A male drama of transgression and punishment thus lies behind the composition of *Bernarda Alba*, in which the mother has no desire and the daughter Adela is punished by death for her sexuality. However, if the play insists even here in a world of women on the persistence of men as objects of desire (for men are constantly invoked or observed by the sisters), then the drama represented on stage is one of rivalry between sisters for an absent male, a rivalry on which the spectator's erotic interest is focused.

I shall argue then that in its very insistence on the inescapability of male mediation *Bernarda Alba* creates a space, perilous and provisional, in which desiring relations between women can be drawn into visibility. But let us first examine three scenes from Mario Camus's film version of *Bernarda Alba*.[8]

García Lorca's play begins inside Bernarda's house and does not leave it for the duration of the drama. Camus chooses, mistakenly perhaps, to open out the beginning and establish the characters within the setting of the church in which the funeral of Bernarda's husband is taking place.[9] In the first sequence of the film a master shot of the village leads to a brief exterior of the church. Camus then cuts to an extreme close-up of Bernarda's stick. Close-ups follow of the faces of each of the daughters in turn, ending with Ana Belén's Adela (Plate 1).[10] These are crosscut with a slow tracking shot up the nave towards the altar. The black dresses of the women contrast with the golden ornaments of the church. Soon afterwards this camera movement is repeated, but from a higher angle. In a rare crane shot the camera moves forward to the altar once more over the heads of the congregation and descends behind Bernarda. She turns and advances straight to the camera, which retreats before her back down the nave as the daughters fall in behind. The women disappear into shadow.[11]

Cinematography and editing serve here to establish the family as an allegory of power relations. As the spectator approaches the drama (as the camera moves closer to the women) each daughter is shown to be subject to the phallus (the stick held by Bernarda). Indeed, we are shown the stick before we are shown any of the women. The framing of each daughter on her own in close-up emphasizes their isolation; the long, unbroken take in which the camera swoops down behind Bernarda only to be swept forward in front of her stresses the omnipotence of the matriarch, queen of all she surveys. By extending the action beyond the family home, Camus sabotages the claustrophobia on which the original play depends; but by establishing Bernarda's mastery within the setting of a church, he suggests that the matriarch does not act in isolation, that her tyranny reproduces and redirects male institutions outside the home.

A little later in Act 1 Bernarda is serving lemonade to a group of mourners in her house. As she reads a litany for her dead husband, cinematic technique once more reinforces the spectator's perception of power relations amongst women and between women and men. Camus crosscuts between close-ups of Bernarda and her daughters and then follows the eldest, Angustias, as she spies on the men outside in the corral. The male mourners are seen in a subjective or point-of-view shot as if by the woman spying from behind the window. Men, who do not appear on stage in García Lorca's original, will be glimpsed in Camus's film version only, as here, in blurred and indistinct form and always from a woman's perspective. The camera thus attempts to reproduce that identification of the spectators in the audience with the (female) spectators within the play on which García Lorca's *Bernarda Alba* relies. By positioning the cinema audience in the place of the desiring woman, the film (re)produces the equivalence of look and desire (of vision and passion) on which a dominant cinema is founded.

Let us examine a final sequence: the climactic scene of the play in which Ana Belén's Adela and Victoria Peña's Martirio confess to each other their common love for the same man (Plate 2). What interests me here is that their dialogue is shot not (as one would expect) in reverse angle close-ups of each actor, but in a single long take in which both women remain in frame as the camera moves around them. The sequence is lit, unusually, with a non-naturalistic blue light.

Women's sexuality is hardly autonomous here; rather it is wholly subordinated to the power of an absent male. However, that male does not appear in the sequence. The spectator is thus left with visual evidence of the erotic rivalry amongst women, a rivalry at least as intense as their common desire for a man. One line of the play cut by Camus from this sequence is Martirio's: 'Even if I wanted to see you as a sister, now I can only see you as a woman.' The cut line suggests not only the question of visibility, of new and different ways of seeing the same relation, but also that the incest taboo is suspended, the family infused with forbidden erotic drives.

Yet in general Camus's film lacks almost completely the spiralling dramatic intensity of García Lorca's original. Soft-focus photography,[12] delicately diffused lighting and antiquarian art design combine to form a languorous aestheticism and timid naturalism.[13] It is a style typical of Camus's literary adaptations, a style promoted as exemplary by Pilar Miró, one-time head of film production at the Ministry of Culture. The hidden history of

Camus's *Bernarda Alba* is that of a Socialist government which sponsored a cinema intended to mirror its own consensus politics, a cinema specializing in adaptations of literary classics with unimpeachable anti-authoritarian credentials. However, as John Hopewell notes of another of Camus's adaptations, unless culture is extended to include 'the ugly and the awkward' the films produced will continue to be visually pleasing whatever the cost to the original material.[14] The glossy production values of Camus's *Bernarda Alba* are thus not merely the result of an individual director's artistic temperament; they also betray the ideological commitment of the Spanish government to the celebration of a certain cultural heritage.

I have suggested that certain sequences of Camus's film do provide cinematic equivalents of García Lorca's dramatic techniques by reassigning the gaze and spectatorial identification of dominant cinema to women. But if we look more closely at what Camus omits from the play, another pattern emerges. Thus, in the litany sequence, Lorca's Bernarda sings out the words and does not merely recite them; and in the confession sequence, Martirio urges her sister to 'plunge a knife into her' if she wishes. Absent from the dialogue in both sequences are diminutives: Lorca's Bernarda speaks of 'lucecitas' (little lights), his Adela of 'una casita' (a little house). Camus consistently omits those elements of dialogue or performance which are most extravagant or lyrical or which point (like the diminutive) to idiosyncratic or regionalist readings. He also cuts moments of incongruous humour: just before the litany Bernarda states that women in church should look at no man but the priest and at him only because he wears a skirt (p. 11). Camus's naturalism cannot assimilate those aspects of García Lorca's theatre which go beyond dour documentary realism, which exceed his own ambition of reproducing the real. He is thus driven to excise all formal extravagance, all disruption of the theatrical or cinematic apparatus. The melodramatic excesses of the play prove profoundly embarrassing.

And it is here, in the identification of textual excess with female sexuality, that *Bernarda Alba* links up with de Lauretis's account of sexual indifference. The action of the play suggests the Platonic standard, according to which 'in the absence of men, women's sexual functioning is aimless and unproductive, merely a form of rottenness and decay' and within which there is an 'interdependence of sexual and reproductive faculties' ('Sexual

Indifference', pp. 157–8): Adela's life is sterile until she is impregnated by Pepe. However, this 'indissoluble knot of sexuality and reproduction' (p. 159), characteristic of the gendered sexuality projected on to women by men, is called into question by the play's twin, contradictory attempts to escape gender: first, by disguising its specificity (reading the sisters as universal subjects, generalizable victims of repression); second, by embracing and exaggerating gender, in the contrast between the wayward hysteria of the daughters and the inflexible masculinity of the mother, fused with her phallus-stick. The continued insistence on gender, as residue of sexual difference, even in a woman's world, thus suggests that sexual similarity cannot be simply seen (and hence eroticized), that the critical and formal work of the text (manifest in García Lorca, veiled in Camus) may be more important than its overt content.

Moreover, the monstrous figure of Bernarda remains, clearly exceeding all naturalistic motivation, outstripping Irene Gutiérrez Caba's somewhat muted performance (Plate 3). And if we look at the development of Spanish cinema we see that García Lorca's devouring matriarch haunts filmmakers, who return constantly to the scene of her crimes.

John Hopewell notes that in contrast to a Republican cinema which emphasized community values, 'under Franco the essential social nucleus became the family and the most used setting the interior of a mansion belonging to the upper class' (*Out of the Past*, p. 16). Filmmakers critical of the regime (such as Camus in the sixties) adopted the elliptical style known later as the 'Francoist aesthetic', characterized by 'metaphor, symbol, allegory . . . and subjectivism' (p. 77). Hopewell singles out Camus's *Los farsantes* (The Actors, 1963) and his version of Calderón's *El alcalde de Zalamea* (The Mayor of Zalamea, 1972). The latter, a family drama turning on the rape of a daughter, shows how even conservative classics were open to discreet redirection in the allegorical mode by an oppositional director.

Hopewell entitles his chapter on film of the transition to democracy 'Saying a Long Goodbye to Mother'. Quotes from the major directors of the seventies show how they repeatedly identify gender and nationality, the matriarch and the authoritarian state. Thus Carlos Saura (best known in the UK for his flamenco trilogy of the eighties) claims that his mother forbade any talk of politics, religion or sex in the house, just like the Francoist censor (p. 78). In Saura's *Ana y los lobos* (Ana and the Wolves, 1972) a tyrannical mother dominates her three sons, who represent militarism, lechery and religious hypocrisy. Eventually they rape and murder the young woman who has come to their house as a governess. José Luis Borau's *Furtivos* (Poachers, 1975) takes poaching as a metaphor for Francoism. An incestuous mother is shot dead by her son. Borau compares her to Saturn devouring his children: she is 'Spain itself who wants her children only for herself, who loves, crushes and devours them' (p. 100). Ricardo Franco's *Pascual Duarte* (also made in 1975, the year of Franco's death, but not released until 1976) features another matricidal son, described by the director as a 'precultural being' who embraces violence as the 'only expressive language of those who have no other means of expression' (p. 129).

Surprisingly, such allegories continue into the democratic era. Saura's sequel to *Ana* is *Mamá cumple cien años* (Mama Turns One Hundred, 1979) in which the grotesquely aged matriarch is betrayed by a family now motivated more by economic than ideological interests. For Julio Pérez Perucha, Mama is the spirit of Francoism personified (Hopewell, p. 148). In all these tragedies of enclosed spaces, family relationships are based not on affection but on power hierarchies; that is, the home serves as an allegory of 'an authoritarian political order' (p. 139). What these films have in common, then, is a masking of gender by nationality: women are identified in male fantasy with that Francoism under which they suffered more than most. But this projective fantasy also requires a division between sexless or incestuous older women (like Bernarda) and younger, sexually active women (like Adela) who are punished by death for their desire. Women are thus made to figure both repression and licence, the evils of dictatorship and the perils of democracy. But what if the matriarch is granted autonomous sexuality? And what if the object of her desire is not the son but the daughter? This is the question posed by Almodóvar's *Entre tinieblas* of 1983.

3. *ENTRE TINIEBLAS* (DARK HABITS): CINEMA AND VISIBILITY

Bernarda's house is compared by La Poncia to a convent (p. 46). Almodóvar's setting is quite literally a convent and his film was shot entirely in an authentic location on the calle Hortaleza in central Madrid (Plate 4). Nuria Vidal has pointed out the formal structure of the plot of this, Almodóvar's third feature.[15] She writes that it consists of a prologue, three acts and an epilogue (p. 285). The prologue finds Yolanda, a nightclub singer, alone at night in an inhospitable Madrid after the accidental overdose of her lover. As she takes refuge from the police in the convent, Act 1 establishes Yolanda's dependence on the Mother Superior (played by the excellent Julieta Serrano)[16] for supplies of heroin and the Mother Superior's dependence on Yolanda for emotional satisfaction. Act 2 stages the women's separation: Yolanda withdraws from heroin; the Mother Superior attempts to distance herself from the younger woman who does not reciprocate her love. Act 3 consists of an unlikely fiesta in the convent at which Yolanda sings a song of farewell to the Mother Superior. The brief epilogue is a scene of amorous desolation in which the Mother Superior realizes she has been abandoned by Yolanda.

As in García Lorca, then, this is a drama set amongst women: the brief incursions of men into the convent have little effect and the only regular male visitor is a priest who (as Almodóvar says) is feminized because he 'wears a skirt' (Vidal, p. 88). And, as in García Lorca once more, power relations between the sexes are redistributed amongst members of the same sex: the Mother Superior attempts to retain her authority over an eccentric group of nuns (a sleazy novelist, an ex-murderess, a seamstress, a housekeeper with a pet tiger).

Actress Julieta Serrano claims that the convent is a utopian space outside Spanish society (Vidal, p. 69). However, this disavowal of history is contradicted by a number of factors. The first is the persistent tendency we have seen in Spanish cinema to read such households allegorically as (in the words of filmmaker Manuel Gutiérrez Aragón) 'a microscopic state . . . a summary of the tensions and structures' of the nation (Hopewell, p. 194). The second factor is the reception of the film itself. On its release in 1983 its apparent anticlericalism aroused fierce controversy at the Venice Film Festival and provoked bomb threats from neo-Fascists to cinemas in Madrid where it was playing.[17] Almodóvar himself has claimed that the film is not scandalous, that he sought not to shock his audience but to establish a relation of complicity with it (Vidal, p. 70). But it is in this complicity that the film's political dimension lies. For the matter-of-fact depiction of drug abuse and lesbianism amongst nuns suggests a libertarian ethic typical of post-Franco Spain, an ethic in which the audience must acquiesce lest it be accused of authoritarianism. It is a typical irony, however, that a director who has always prided himself on being 'the most modern man in Madrid' should express that modernity in the genre of the religious film (typical of Francoism)[18] and in the figure of a Mother Superior (traditional agent of authority). Hence, in its very disavowal of Spanish history *Entre tinieblas* testifies to the political culture under which it was made and to the ambiguous relation of that culture to the dictatorship that preceded it.

In *Bernarda Alba* women compete for the love of a man who remains outside the house; in *Entre tinieblas* they are rivals for the affections of a woman who is lodged temporarily within it. I suggest in a moment that it is at the level of cinematic technique rather than content that Almodóvar inscribes a new frame of visibility for relations between women. However, it is important to note that on the film's release male critics were unable to see the love story which Nuria Vidal rightly claims as central to the film's narrative structure. By closing their eyes to the Mother Superior's desire, such critics also mistake the film's genre, dismissing it as a farce. Julieta Serrano, however, has repeatedly stressed the seriousness of both her performance as the Mother Superior and Almodóvar's cinematic ambitions in the film, claiming that both went unrecognized at the time (p. 92). If García Lorca is more playful than is generally acknowledged, lacing even the tragic *Bernarda Alba* with melodramatic motifs, Almodóvar is more serious, interrupting his crazy comedy with unambiguously tragic moments.

With its claustrophobic interiors and monochrome costumes, *Entre tinieblas* is visually closer to García Lorca's *Bernarda Alba* than to Mario Camus's de luxe film version. But the aesthetic qualities of *Entre tinieblas* reflect economic restrictions as much as artistic choices. Shooting in natural interiors with restricted opportunities for cinematography and editing is typical of Spanish filmmaking from the 1970s to 1983, when the so-called Miró law ushered in a period of more generous government subsidy. And until the massive international success of *Mujeres al borde de un ataque de nervios* (Women on the Verge of a Nervous Breakdown, 1989) Almodóvar was not as favoured as other directors by the Spanish establishment. However, Almodóvar does make use at some points in *Entre tinieblas* of techniques used later by Camus in

Bernarda Alba, though to markedly different effect, and he does so at similar points in his narrative. We can thus examine three sequences once more, parallel to those in *Bernarda Alba*: a scene in a chapel; the recitation of a litany; and a declaration of love.

The chapel scene initiates Act 1 of the film. The six nuns, seen in long shot, rise to their feet and walk down the nave towards the camera. Behind them the doors open on to the street and light floods in. Almodóvar cuts to medium close-ups of the Mother Superior and Yolanda. In an aerial (crane) shot the Mother Superior walks away from the camera towards the source of the light, which casts a halo around the new arrival. The camera then follows the Mother Superior in a lateral tracking shot until Yolanda comes into frame on the left.[19]

As Almodóvar himself notes, this sequence is a 'transparent metaphor'. Yolanda's arrival is a 'divine apparition', which embodies 'the sacredness of human love' (Vidal, p. 75). Almodóvar goes on to claim that 'there is a straight line which goes from Yolanda to the altar and this path, which [the Mother Superior] follows, is the axis of the film'. It is also, we might add, the axis down which the camera shoots from the crane and along which it travels in the subsequent tracking shot. The linearity of cinematography and editing here thus mirrors the symbolic vector of the sequence, which suggests an equivalence between religious and secular passion. In a film of frequent high angles,[20] which tend to trap the women in confined spaces, pinning them to the floor (Vidal, p. 67), this crane shot suggests rather a transcendent position from which women achieve a divine viewpoint.

The redirection of Catholic iconography (of dominant ways of seeing) recurs in a litany sequence. As Sister Rat (played by Chus Lampreave) reads a text on the dangers of kissing, the camera moves in a very slow tracking shot past the faces of each nun in turn, revealing their respective reactions: delighted, depressed, suspicious. It comes to rest on the rapt face of the Mother Superior, who we know is thinking of Yolanda. Note once more the frontal setup with each woman facing the camera straight on. The chiaroscuro lighting is also important here. In a typically eclectic move, Almodóvar claims to have modelled lighting effects on both Zurbarán (Spanish painter of the seventeenth century) and Douglas Sirk (director of Hollywood melodramas in the 1950s) (Vidal, p. 73) (Plate 5).[21] The text read by Sister Rat was not written for the film but is an authentic religious tract of the

1960s called *La doncella cristiana* (The Christian Maiden).[22] As Almodóvar remarks, the lush sensuality of its language is caused by the attempt to prohibit an erotic practice which it succeeds only in rendering all the more attractive (Vidal, p. 102). Once more the film's relation to Spanish history is ambiguous here. It at once invokes the repressions of the Francoist era and slyly suggests that they have no purchase on the present. Almodóvar, a very vocal critic of the treatment he received at the hands of the priests whose school he attended, here seeks to establish a more subtle relation of complicity with the spectator. The sequence suggests (disingenuously perhaps) that past prohibitions may be disavowed, that they are simply a source of pleasure for the secular, libertarian society which can exploit them as it wishes.

We come now to a final sequence which Almodóvar has called 'a perfect declaration of love' (Vidal, p. 104). Yolanda enters the Mother Superior's office wearing a red shirt and grey trousers. As she draws nearer to the Mother Superior, seated at a desk, Almodóvar crosscuts between the two women as they sing along to a bolero by Latin American Lucho Gatica, 'Encadenados' (In Chains). The faces grow larger in the frame; but they also turn to face the camera directly. The women thus sing to each other; but they also sing out to the spectator in the audience, who is confronted by a direct address infrequent in conventional cinema. The audience is thus positioned in the unaccustomed place of the desiring woman.

Almodóvar has written humorously that Lucho Gatica composed this song several decades ago with his film in mind (Vidal, p. 104). As we saw in the case of Catholic iconography elsewhere in the film, the meaning of preexisting imagery is subtly changed when placed within a new context.[23] Just as Adela's declaration of love appeals to religious language (she identifies herself as a fallen woman with Christ), so the Mother Superior's declaration is made through secular imagery, through popular music which (the characters claim) 'speaks of the feelings . . . tells the truth about life'. Habitually, Almodóvar uses music against image as a counterpoint or ironic commentary. Here, however, music and image coincide, each reinforcing the effect of the other.

What is this effect? I would suggest that by framing relations between women in a new way the sequence not only points to an autonomous form of female sexuality; it also suggests a strategy of representation that alters the standard of vision familiar from Hollywood cinema. To cite Teresa de Lauretis once more, *Entre tinieblas* offers us:

> the place of a woman who desires another woman; the place from where each one looks at the other with desire and, more important still, a place from where we see their look and their desire, a place where the equivalence of look and desire – which sustains spectatorial pleasure and the very power of cinema in constructing and orienting the viewer's identification – is invested in two women. ('Film and the Visible', p. 227)

It is hardly surprising that male critics have chosen not to see this space; it is remarkable that a director often accused of misogyny should have produced such a sequence.

I would argue, then, that Almodóvar coincides here with de Lauretis's prescriptions for dislodging the erotic from the discourse on gender: through music and *mise-en-scène*, through cutting and camera placement Almodóvar 'undomesticates the woman's body' which is 'reinscribed in excess, as excess' ('Sexual Indifference', p. 165). And he does so not only by dissolving the male-projected knot of sexuality and reproduction (Yolanda, unlike Adela, is not impregnated by her boyfriend, who dies as the film begins), but also by parodically embracing sexual difference in the visual and chromatic contrast between the exhibitionistic Yolanda, in her scarlet blouse, and the Mother Superior, modest in her black habit. It is not enough, then, simply to represent sexual similarity (a woman who sees and desires another woman): any film with oppositional ambitions must work also and more urgently to undo any 'compliance with the apparatus of commercial cinema and its institutional drive to, precisely, commodity exchange' (p. 173). Only then can gender be, momentarily, escaped and spectatorial expectations redirected.

4. THE PASSION OF THE MOTHER

I mentioned earlier that Mario Camus systematically cuts those excessive or superfluous details of García Lorca's text which make *Bernarda Alba* a melodrama, those moments which frustrate the naturalist ambition of reproducing the real. We have seen that Almodóvar, like Lorca, exploits a performative surplus, an appeal to the expressive potential of language and cinema which transcends what is strictly necessary for narrative purposes: stylized camerawork, dramatic lighting, lushly sensual text and music. This is not, however, to claim that such formal techniques are inherently progressive or oppositional. What interests me here is the combination of those techniques with the new version of the matriarchal figure who (as we have seen) haunts Spanish cinema under and after Franco. Most filmmakers follow García Lorca in contrasting a sexless and ruthless dictator with an impassioned daughter. Almodóvar, however, transfers the daughter's passion to the mother, thus eroticizing the enclosed space she controls. There is a triple movement at work here. Almodóvar at first disavows Spanish history, refusing to refer to Francoism in his films or to acknowledge political readings of them. At the same time, however, he repeats a dominant metaphor of twentieth-century Spanish narrative: the matriarchal family as allegory of the state. But in this new version for the 1980s the mother is passionate and vulnerable. Almodóvar has claimed that his ninth film *Tacones lejanos* (High Heels, 1991) was originally based on *Bernarda Alba* (Vidal, p. 251). But it is not *Tacones lejanos* but *Entre tinieblas* that reworks *Bernarda Alba*, repeating and redirecting the mother–daughter relation, working through the old story once more, but with feeling.

We have seen that other male artists project the omnipotence of the historical father/fascist on to a mythical phallic mother. Such strategies reveal not only the mobility of subject positions in fantasy, but also the inextricability of fantasy and politics. If the Englishman's home is his castle, the Spaniard's home is (in John Hopewell's image) an arena in which the spectacles of gender, nationality and sexuality are represented, in which both fully social and unconscious drives are played out. My reading of García Lorca and Almodóvar has also proposed that the study of theatre and cinema (of all cultural production) must be at once and alternately historical and theoretical. For there can be no history innocent of theoretical bias, no theory untouched by historical determination.

Almodóvar's early films have been much criticized for lack of dramatic development.[24] And in the desolation of the Mother Superior, as in the suicide of Adela, we might see a certain inertia that in Gaylyn Studlar's words can be 'resolved only in death', that 'signals the collapse of conventional narrativity ... which leads progressively to an endpoint of satisfying resolution'.[25] The spiralling narratives of both *Bernarda Alba* and *Entre tinieblas* are based not so much on mechanisms of cause and effect as on patterns of repetition, for Studlar 'a key formal structure of masochism'. Many women will not see masochist abjection as a fruitful solution to the double movement of projection and reabsorption by which men create a 'feminine character' in their own image. I would argue, however, that the process of projection is so clear in García Lorca and Almodóvar that it betrays its own makers. As de Lauretis has argued of Fellini, that other fantasist of excess, 'his representation of gender is so transparent as to reveal, in the very image of woman, the massive narrative shadow of [the director] in drag.'[26] Abjection or transvestism: two techniques (two strategies) to render the invisible visible. They suggest, in their discomfort, even in their absurdity, that like J.B. Trend in a Granadine garden many years ago, we may strive once more with attention, once more with feeling, to hear what has not been heard, to see what has not been seen, to change the very conditions of visibility.

NOTES

1 J.B. Trend, *Lorca and the Spanish Poetic Tradition* (Oxford: Basil Blackwell, 1956), pp. 1–2.

2 Teresa de Lauretis, 'Sexual Indifference and Lesbian Representation', *Theatre Journal* 40 (1988), pp. 155–77; see also 'Film and the Visible', in Bad Object Choices [sic], eds, *How Do I Look?: Queer Film and Video* (Seattle: Bay Press, 1991), pp. 223–64.

3 Camus graduated from the Escuela Oficial de Cinematografía; he is perhaps best known for the TV version of the classic novel *Fortunata y Jacinta* and for a number of cinematic adaptations of the 1980s, including *La colmena* (The Beehive, 1982) and *Los santos inocentes* (The Holy Innocents, 1984).

4 Here I find myself in rare disagreement with Vicente Molina Foix, who praises Camus's *Bernarda Alba* for its theatrical stylization and wilfully artificial set design and lighting; see his collected reviews in *El cine estilográfico* (Barcelona: Anagrama, 1993), pp. 260–1.

5 Page references are to Federico García Lorca, *La casa de Bernarda Alba*, ed. H. Ramsden (Manchester: Manchester University Press, 1983). Translations are my own.

6 Ian Gibson, *Federico García Lorca: A Life* (London: Faber, 1989).

7 For a subtle and persuasive critique of the literalism of Gibson's biography see Luis Fernández Cifuentes's review of the Spanish edition in *Nueva Revista de Filología* 34 (1985–6), pp. 224–32.

8 For Spanish trade reports on this film see *Cineinforme* 509–10 (April–May 1987), pp. 4–7; 511–12 (May–June 1987), pp. 14–15; 544 (October 1988), pp. 19, 32–3. For the US trade view see *Variety* (20 May 1987), p. 18. For British press reviews see *Monthly Film Bulletin* 674 (March 1990), p. 63; *City Limits* (1 March 1990), p. 33; *Time Out* (28 February 1990), p. 36. Camus's film was networked on UK TV's BBC 2 on 14 February 1992.

9 Camus is perhaps attempting to forestall criticism of 'theatricality'; when *Bernarda Alba* was shown at the London Film Festival the programme notes claimed that 'filmed theatre' was generally 'appalling'; *Official Programme: 31st London Film Festival* (London: BFI, 1987), p. 95.

10 Belén had previously been directed by Camus in the TV *Fortunata y Jacinta* (1979); her persona as a self-confident and politically progressive woman, who combines careers in popular music, theatre and television with cinema, coloured Spanish audiences' response to her Adela.

11 Vicente Molina Foix also draws attention to this opening sequence, noting that it suggests the 'union' of religion and matriarchy (*El cine*, p. 261).

12 Veteran cinematographer Fernando Arribas had worked with Camus on the TV series *Los desastres de la guerra* (The Disasters of War, 1983); he began his career in documentaries for the Francoist Ministry of Information and Tourism; see Francisco Llinás, *Directores de fotografía del cine español* (Madrid: Filmoteca, 1989), p. 376.

13 A prestigious Spanish critic such as Augusto M. Torres praises the 'sobriety' of the film; *Diccionario del cine español* (Madrid: Espasa Calpe, 1994), p. 138.

14 John Hopewell, *Out of the Past: Spanish Cinema After Franco* (London: BFI, 1986), p. 227.

15 Nuria Vidal, *El cine de Pedro Almodóvar* (Barcelona: Destino, 1988). For Spanish, French and British reactions to this film see my *Laws of Desire: Questions of Homosexuality in Spanish Writing and Film 1960–90* (Oxford: Oxford University Press, 1992), pp. 180–8; and my *Desire Unlimited: The Cinema of Pedro Almodóvar* (London: Verso, 1994), pp. 23–36.

16 According to an interview in Vidal (*El cine*, p. 81), Julieta Serrano was rehearsing for a García Lorca play (*Doña Rosita la soltera*) during the shoot for *Entre tinieblas*.

17 See review by Francisco Marinero in *Diario 16* (8 October 1983).

18 For religious cinema of the 1950s see Carlos F. Heredero's excellent *Las huellas del tiempo: cine español 1951–61* (Madrid: Filmoteca, 1993), pp. 193–203. One antecedent of *Entre tinieblas* discussed by Heredero is Rafael Gil's *Sor Intrépida*, in which a singing nun is dispatched as a missionary to foreign parts, where she is killed by the locals (like one of

Almodóvar's characters). Some of the most popular religious films were based on Palacio Valdés's novel *La hermana San Sulpicio*, which treats the relationship between a doctor and a novice nun; Torres (*Diccionario*, p. 244) lists four versions: 1927, 1934, 1952, 1971.

19 Cinematography is by Angel Luis Fernández, who worked on all of Almodóvar's films from *Laberinto de pasiones* (Labyrinth of Passion, 1982) to *La ley del deseo* (The Law of Desire, 1987). Fernández is also known for his photography on the Madrid comedies of Fernando Colomo and Fernando Trueba; see Llinás, *Directores de fotografía*, pp. 419–20.

20 Molina Foix cites Almodóvar's use of high angles (*picados*) for affective emphasis in his review of the later *Matador* (1986); *El cine estilográfico*, p. 108.

21 The best account of Almodóvar's much-debated relation to Sirkian melo-drama remains Molina Foix's review of *Tacones lejanos* (High Heels, 1991) in *El cine estilográfico*, pp. 110–12. In his earlier review of *Entre tinieblas* Molina Foix had criticized Almodóvar for being too ironic and for lacking the 'naiveté' necessary for true melodrama (*El cine*, p. 196).

22 For an anthology of often grotesque Francoist pedagogy, published in an Almodóvarian spirit of humour and exorcism, see Andrés Sopeña Monsalve, *El florido pensil: memoria de la escuela nacionalcatólica* (Barcelona: Crítica, 1994).

23 For an account of *Entre tinieblas* which links the equation of eroticism and mysticism to the 'dark night' of the film's art design see Víctor Fuentes, 'El cine de Almodóvar y la posmodernidad española (logros y límites)', in George Cabello Castellet, Jaume Martí-Olivella and Guy H. Wood, eds, *Cine-Lit: Essays on Peninsular Film and Fiction* (Corvallis/Portland: Oregon State/Portland State/Reed College, 1992), p. 216.

24 See, for example, Torres (*Diccionario*, p. 66).

25 Gaylyn Studlar, *In the Realm of Pleasure: Von Sternberg, Dietrich, and the Masochistic Aesthetic* (New York: Columbia University Press, 1988), p. 123.

26 Teresa de Lauretis, *Technologies of Gender: Essays on Theory, Film, and Fiction* (London: Macmillan, 1987), p. xi.

2

KIKA:

Vision Machine

1. SIGHTLESS VISION

One photograph; three captions. The photograph: Pedro Almodóvar peeking out from between scarlet curtains, a green, spotted bow in his black curly hair. The captions: 'Genius or hype?' (*El País Semanal*, Madrid);[1] 'Ready for our closeup?' (*Out*, New York);[2] 'I feel like a carnival freak' (*Observer*, London).[3] This publicity shot for *Kika* recapitulates the three issues which, I have argued, are fundamental for any understanding of the cinema of Pedro Almodóvar.[4] The very visible bow is the sign of a conspicuous visual pleasure coded as feminine in film theory. The polka dots or *lunares* on the bow and curtains function as a parodic pointer to Spanishness, to the *españolada*.[5] And the adoption by a man of this flamboyant femininity serves as an index of homosexuality, defined here not as desire for the same sex, but as identification with the other.[6] Beyond these references to gender, nationality and homosexuality, however, the photograph is framed by the captions which give evidence of the audiences by which *Kika* was received. The Spanish caption testifies to the continuing debate over the artistic value of the nation's most commercially successful filmmaker; the North American invites a metropolitan gay readership to recognize itself in a camp quotation;[7] the British objectifies the filmmaker, confining him and his work to an exotic and eccentric space from which the UK general public is safely insulated.

Problematization, identification, objectification: the different press framings of a single image remind us that the social reception of cinema cannot be dissociated from the work itself, that the tributary media actively serve to produce a multiplicity of audiences for a filmic work. More importantly, perhaps, the publicity shot suggests an instantaneous redoubling or con/fusion of presentation and representation typical of Almodóvar's cinema. Simultaneously director and actor, Almodóvar presides over a proliferating series of discrete images typified by the grid on the film's poster, in which each actor is isolated in a repeated pattern of high-definition fluorescent colour shot against a white background. Once more the graphic style (by long-time collaborator Juan Gatti) con/fuses presentation and representation: contact-sheet-format publicity material (captioned by *Out* 'Pedro's People') extends the aesthetics of the film itself to members of the production company and others who have contributed to Almodóvar's career over the last decade. In this parade of phatic images, whose purpose is simply to 'force [the viewer] to look, to hold his or her attention',[8] designer, actor, make-up artist and publicity person, each is indistinguishable from the other.

This triumph of design in Almodóvar is hardly news. What I will suggest in this chapter, however, is that the logic or paralogic of the publicity shot is symptomatic of what French cultural theorist Paul Virilio has called 'the vision machine', a regime of ever-increasing visibility which leads, paradoxically, to an aesthetics of disappearance or of blindness, which is 'the result of an ever brighter illumination, of the intensity of definition' (*Vision*, p. 14). At the opening party for *Kika* in London, an event dense with fashionable trademarks (from the locale itself to the free food and drink served in the VIP section), Almodóvar was accompanied by models dressed in the Jean-Paul Gaultier costumes worn by Victoria Abril's character in the film.[9] The costumes, subsequently auctioned for an AIDS charity, thus substituted for the bodies of the actors who had worn them. There could be no more transparent emblem of what Virilio has called the 'disidentified image', a certain 'waning of reality' produced by the 'instrumental splitting of modes of perception and representation' (p. 49). But that 'passage from vision to visualization' (p. 13) exemplified by Almodóvar's fashion-conscious identity parades is also, and quite explicitly, the object of critique within *Kika*. And, as in Virilio's *The Vision Machine*, in *Kika* the con/fusion of presentation and

representation (the shift from the dialectical duration to the paradoxical instant) is related to the decline of cinema and the rise
of video. Let us, then, suspend the questions of audience and
reception to which I referred above and of which I have written
elsewhere[10] and take seriously the critique of reproductive technology we find in *Kika*, reading it not as a topical intervention
in the debate on Spanish media in the nineties (although clearly
it is), but rather as a comment on and a symptom of that depersonalization of vision and duplication of the body which
follows in the wake of the vision machine.[11]

Kika's credit sequence begins with a keyhole, a camera shutter
and a woman undressing. On a shoot for a lingerie spread,
mother-obsessed photographer Ramón (Alex Casanovas) pleads
with his model to exhibit 'authentic' sexual pleasure for the lens.
It is, however, Ramón whose pleasure must always be mediated by
visual prosthesis. Fumbling with voyeuristic delight over the bored
model's body, he represents that distancing teletopology which
for Virilio 'anticipates human movement, outstripping every
displacement of the body' (p. 6). Once 'the visual field is reduced
to that of a sighting device' (p. 13) (a process which the cinema
audience is invited to share), then the subject is absent from
the scene of his sight. Contradicting the reality principle that
'Everything I see is . . . within my reach' (p. 7), the reality effect
of the new logistics of perception abstracts the body of the
witness, 'delocalizing geometrical optics' (p. 12): a later shot in
the sequence reveals that the model is not, as we had thought,
lying supine on a bed, but is rather standing against a vertical
mock up.

Kika's temporal frame is as disorientating as its spatial optic.
Flashing forward from the opening time frame in which Ramón
discovers his mother's supposed suicide to the present in which
Kika addresses her cosmetics class on the glory of the false eyelash
(Plate 6), the plot immediately flashes back once more to the
televized book promotion in which Nicholas (Peter Coyote) plugs
his autobiographical novel on a show presented (or, as she puts it,
'represented') by Almodóvar's own mother, Francisca Caballero,
and to Kika's inadvertent resurrection of the narcoleptic Ramón
as she attempts to 'give back natural colour' to a corpse. While
the TV show juxtaposes a parodically heightened regionalism
(Manchegan *mise-en-scène*) with the delocalized modernity and
internationalism of a US author (and actor, dubbed by a Spaniard),

the resurrection scene also laments the loss of a social or familial sphere in the supposed 'Americanization' of a solitary wake without family or friends. If here the cosmetic is indistinguishable from the organic (is Ramón's flush natural or artificial?), then Ramón's narcolepsy, the con/fusion of life and death, is also the inversion of an order of perception: the close-up of his blank, unseeing look signals a new sightless vision in an age when 'objects perceive us' (p. 59), when, in Virilio's words, 'the human eye no longer gives signs of recognition, no longer organises the search for truth' (p. 43).

Nicholas's subsequent arrival at the sterile new Atocha station also hints at this 'topographical amnesia' in which the body's lived relation to a duration of space and sight is lost. But Virilio's 'permanent regime of bedazzlement', his intuition that 'the most distinctive cities [in this case Madrid] bear within them the capacity of being nowhere' (p. 10), is most spectacularly borne out by the sequences taken from the real-life crime show 'The Worst of the Day', hosted by Victoria Abril's Andrea Caracortada. Here Gaultier's celebrated costumes pose or expose the supplementary status of the body in the vision machine: exploding prosthetic breasts pierce the skintight surface of a black gown, dappled with plastic blood (Plate 7); body parts (eyes, ears, breasts) are redoubled by electronic prostheses (video, audio, lighting) fused with a black rubber epidermis. As substitute for the body's waning powers and as addition to traditional human faculties, the costumes parade that instrumentalization of the senses that Virilio both laments and celebrates. It is an instrumentalization re-inforced by Almodóvar's (or Alfredo Mayo's)[12] shooting style. Thus Andrea's video footage of everyday horrors (the on-camera murder of a mother in a cemetery) is offered to us from the ambiguous point of view, at once objective and subjective, of the cyborg camera costume. And wilfully con/fusing presentation and representation Andrea is (like Almodóvar in the broader spectacle of his cinema) at once actor and director of her horror shows, playing a conspicuous role in them even as she insists she simply reproduces them, mechanically, for the screen. The communal space of a live audience (here reduced to phantasmal empty seats) is displaced by the fragmented electronic audience, the public space by the public image: Andrea delivers one homily while seated on a TV set; the maid (Rossy de Palma) is shot from behind the screen which, in a symptomatic reversal, appears to be watching her. Caught by and in the video frame, bodies no longer inhabit the universe; rather the (electronic) universe inhabits them (p. 27).

But Virilio would argue that this 'perception of special detachment', this 'integrated circuit of vision' and death (p. 38) is not simply the result of technological development or deployment. Rather Andrea's Medusa-look (which dispossesses, blinds, immobilizes) is the terror effect which is the dark shadow of rationality and Enlightenment. The reality show merely mimics that 'illumination of the private sphere', that desire 'to obtain a total image of society by dispersing its dark secrets' (p. 34) deployed by modern governmentality; tracking down darkness, it exhibits both an 'obsession with the unsaid', which demands witnesses be called on to confess, and a 'totalitarian desire for clarification' (p. 34), which demands images be exhibited to the greatest number of citizens. Andrea's advantage, however, is that video permits her a certain compression of time associated with its visual instantaneity (p. 37). It is Virilio's argument (and one confirmed by *Kika*) that when image redoubles object and time space there must be a crisis in media characterized by delay and representation (such as cinema) to the advantage of media devoted to the instant of presentation (such as video). Although Andrea's same-day reportages are not real time, they point to the displacement of past, present and future by a new temporal order of real time and delayed time, of an endlessly repeatable and continuously pending 'latent immediacy' (p. 43).

Two later scenes exemplify the new temporal order of the vision machine. First, when Ramón and Kika attempt unsuccessfully to make love, the former insists on using a polaroid camera as a 'sight line' for his desire, thus bypassing the body. Through a technological 'phenomenon of acceleration' (p. 4), Ramón reduplicates the instant, privileging 'precision of detail' over that 'sharing of duration' necessary for any intersubjective experience. As Rodin said of a photographic model, Ramón is like a 'man suddenly struck with paralysis', his sense of 'felt temporality' lost to the 'image-time-freeze' (p. 2) of the photographer who, unlike the sculptor or painter, does not 'take his body with him' (p. 16). Secondly, and more notoriously, Kika is raped by escaped porno actor Paul Bazzo (*polvazo* = big fuck), a character unable to distinguish between a fictional and an authentic sexual performance, and her violation is replayed on a video submitted by a mysterious voyeur to Andrea's TV show. Here, once more, according to the paradoxical logic of video, a means of action is immediately a means of representation (p. 29). And once more it is a question of detail. Virilio sarcastically cites Benjamin's proposal that photography 'opens up the clear field where all intimacy leads to the clarification of details' (p. 23). The voyeur's attachment to the intensive detail is thus not simply a psychic mechanism; rather it is a technique typical of a society of surveill-ance: 'the elucidation of details [is a] means of governing, [a form of] omnivoyance' (p. 33). It is an omnivoyance characterized by a redoubling of the point of view. In just the same way our initial 'objective' viewpoint of the rape is first subjectivized by the revela-tion that Ramón had been the voyeur who notified the singularly ineffective police, only to be objectivized once more by Andrea's confirmation that the videotape was sent to her by one of her multiple and anonymous voyeuristic collaborators. This is for Virilio precisely the definition of the vision machine: a form of sightless vision or automated perception in which viewpoints are split and perception shared 'between the animate (the living subject) and the inanimate (the object, the seeing machine)' (p. 59). Kika's unknown witness, whose identity and location Almodóvar does not care to elucidate, embodies that depersonalization and delocalization typical of the paradoxical logic of the video era.

The last reel of the film repeats, once more, the redoubling of the look which is also the con/fusion of presentation and representation: Nicholas reveals that he is a serial killer to Andrea and to her camera simultaneously; as he lies dying he offers his fictional manuscript to Kika, assuring her that it will be an auto-biographical bestseller; and when, after multiple murders, Kika exclaims 'How long will this nightmare last?' she echoes a question members of the cinema audience may well be asking themselves. Struggling ever more desperately to bring the body into visibility (displaying repeated frontal nude shots of Bibi Andersen), Almodóvar exhausts his image repertoire, surrendering to the intensity of the phatic image rather than the scope or space of the public image, proving that, when truth is no longer masked but rather eclipsed by its televized image, 'what is perceived is already finished' (p. 69), evacuated by its own luminous velocity.

It is Virilio's contention that the formal logic of eighteenth-century painting or engraving gave way to the dialectical logic of nineteenth-century photography or film, to be displaced itself by the paradoxical logic of video or computer graphics. It is a shift from the real to the actual to the virtual, similar to those traced by other theorists such as Baudrillard. However, Virilio's account of the 'crisis in traditional forms of public representation' suggests that *Kika* is at once a critique and a symptom of the shift from film to video. The supposed 'disaster' of the film (much trumpeted by Spanish critics) thus goes beyond *Kika*'s own undeniable narrative incoherence[13] to speak of the problems of affect, politics and a critical space in the age of the vision machine. Let us begin with affect. For Virilio, the 'hyperrealism' of surveillance procedures (including the law and the police) has led to the devaluation of eyewitness accounts and a putting to death of the body: 'How', he asks, 'can we hope to scandalize, surprise, move to tears before . . . the distant technological outcome of the merciless more light of revolutionary terror?' (p. 44). It is a question burlesqued by Almodóvar himself when he has Andrea warn her audiences that her programme may offend their sensibilities, if they have any left. But it is also a question to be posed to an Almodóvar whose quest to illuminate the bizarre and the novel has now been outstripped by the mainstream TV shows he affects to despise.[14] In a cinema, such as Almodóvar's, in which sensation was always crosscut with sentiment, this exhaustion of affect may prove lethal indeed. The increasingly cursory nature of *Kika*'s detective story (a genre which Virilio associates with the 'instrumentalization of the photographic image' [p. 36]) also bears witness to the decline of narrative in the age of instant video testimony.

The second problem is that of politics. Virilio claims that the temporal mode of film documentaries was that of the 'fatum' or event completed-in-the-past: 'They . . . induced a feeling of the irreparable, and through a dialectical reaction, fostered [the] violent will to engage the future' (p. 25). The instantaneity of video, however, in which the 'presence of the past is [no longer] impressed on plate or film' (p. 64), produces not events but accidents; and its paralogic, outstripping and displacing the felt duration of history, can engender at most a momentary surprise in its mesmerized audience. *Kika* both laments that loss and compulsively repeats it in its neglect of duration or suspense (the police investigation is derisory) and its scorn for psychological depth or motivation (Nicholas's malevolence is unexplained). An unlikely moralizer, Almodóvar can only lay bare the ethical paralysis wrought by the video spectacle; he cannot propose any singular and completed event (certainly not the mediatized rape) which might provoke in his audience the potential for political engagement inspired by the cinema of the past.

Finally there is the question of a critical space. I have argued that *Kika* displays that depersonalized and delocalized perception typical of the phatic image which prizes intensity over extension, immediacy over topographical memory. Virilio goes beyond this, however, arguing that the instrumentalization of vision since photography has radically transformed personal and public perceptions of space and time, citing

> [the] exhaustion of the Cartesian tradition which had sprung out of the original invention of the serialization not only of forms-images but also of mental images and which was the origin of the City and human social communities based on the constitution of collective paramnesias, on the 'ideal of a world essentially the same, essentially shared as that preliminary foundation of the construction of meaning we call geometry'.[15] (p. 27)

Lamenting the loss of the collectivity, both psychic and social, deploring the loss of the City, as a place of imaginary continuity and sameness, *Kika* also uncritically reproduces those losses in its celebration of the unmotivated and dislocated, in its vindication of singularity and surprise. Almodóvar thus privileges speed over space, image over object, costume over body. In the final sequence, neglecting her responsibilities towards the revived Ramón, Kika heads off with a handsome stranger on a new adventure. And the camera tilts down for a final shot of the white line down the centre of the road she is travelling. It is typical of a narrative in which, for all its references to contemporary Madrid, 'the strategic value of speed's "no-place" has definitively outstripped the value of place' (p. 31) and 'seeing the world becomes not only a matter of spatial difference but . . . a matter of speed, of acceleration or deceleration' (p. 21).

Now territorial space has been devalued (now Kika has no home to return to), we are lost in the vision machine with Almodóvar; and we may, like his heroine, feel we have lost our way. But *Kika*'s 'failure' admits no simple solution and is not accidental or singular; rather it points, with characteristic perversity, to a pervasive exhaustion of cinema, one which (for Virilio) can be neither surmounted nor circumvented. The seeing devices which dispense with the body; the permanence of the 'regime of bedazzlement'; the madness and terror which are the fellow travellers of technology (pp. 16, 10, 29): it is enough that Almodóvar should raise such questions; we can hardly expect him to answer them.

2. TECHNOLOGIZING GENDER

For Virilio the vision machine is sexually indifferent: a deployment of light and power (of light as power) to which no agents are assigned and no gendered effects attributed. The exhaustion of cinema and its instruments (the waning of affect, politics and the critical space) effect no specific changes in sexed subjects. But feminists such as de Lauretis have taught us to be suspicious of sexual indifference; and as a text which claims to make women central to its narrative, *Kika*'s approach to gender cannot be neglected. In the second half of this chapter, then, I reread the film in the light of two feminist revisions of the relationship between gender and technology: the first is de Lauretis once more, who (following Foucault and others) argues for a technology of sex and gender in a broad sense, but one which has specific implications for cinema;[16] the second is Donna Haraway, who (as a historian of science) treats the gendering of technology in a more restricted sense, but one which is always alert to the implications for women and Woman.[17] While Haraway is perhaps closer to Virilio's postmodern problematic, de Lauretis coincides with Virilio in her profound mistrust of the spectatorial regime and its varied apparatus.

It is an objection frequently raised by critics that Almodóvar's women are simply projections of the director's own masculine subjectivity.[18] De Lauretis addresses this question of directorial drag in relation to Fellini's *Giulietta degli spiriti* (Juliet of the Spirits, 1964).[19] Here the 'narrative image . . . produced for the film by its title' suggests 'an image of Woman as unique individual and eternal feminine at once' (p. 96): the spectator knows Giulietta to be both the name of Fellini's actress wife, who takes the leading role, and the deathless female partner of Shakespeare's tragedy. Rather similarly the title *Kika* elicits a double response: the childish diminutive infers an affective femininity, but it also cites the name of the director's mother, Francisca, who appears as the chat-show host in the film itself. Kika, then, like Giulietta/Juliet, appears to be the eponymous protagonist of the film; yet in neither case does the woman 'control the images and events of the film and move the plot forward' (p. 102); rather the female character 'poses the question of woman's relation to the image of Woman' as 'self-image' (p. 100). De Lauretis claims that Fellini's heroine is 'stuck with . . . all of [his] own obsessive images' and is simply an 'exploration of [the director's] unconscious femininity' (pp. 102–3).

The analysis would appear to hold for Kika also, who frequently fusses about her self-image, changing costume and hair colour during the course of the film, and can only respond to actions which engulf her (the rape, betrayal by men she loves), never initiating action. Moreover, she is surrounded by sounds and images associated by the viewer with Almodóvar himself: Mexican ballads and domestic appliances; Madrid skylines and telephones. When she exclaims, on seeing Almodóvar's mother on television, 'I love Doña Paquita', she seems simply to have taken up the director's place. As de Lauretis argues of male philosophers who write 'in the feminine mode': 'if [they] can occupy and speak from the position of woman, it is because the position is vacant and, what is more, cannot be claimed by women. . . . The question of woman for [them] is a question of style'.[20] As a make-up artist by profession Kika identifies herself as the very image of aesthetics: in the opening credits actress Verónica Forqué's name is shown over a collage of a rose and a stylized female body of the 1950s. Actor and character are identified as the style of the film itself.

Kika, then, is organicity and corporality, as easily moved to tears as she is to laughter or nausea. But the motif of female impersonation by the male is also parodically played out within the narrative: just as Almodóvar has Kika applaud his own mother, so Nicholas reveals *in extremis* that he is the 'lesbian killer' whose murders he has chronicled in his last novel. Indeed it is possible to read Almodóvar's promotion of the film (which involved his donning of designs based on the costumes of characters both male and female)[21] as a mimicry of that aestheticized relation to self (of gender as self-representation) which condemns Kika to passivity and inaction.

But Kika (like Almodóvar in her place) is not simply acted upon. Rather she occupies that slippery position between the ideal and material which de Lauretis identifies as the subject of feminism: 'not only distinct from Woman with a capital letter . . . but also distinct from women, the real, historical beings . . . defined by the technology of gender'.[22] And this trauma of gender is nowhere more visible than in the extended and controversial rape scene. Almodóvar has consistently claimed that this sequence is proof of Kika's strength, not weakness: her vigorous resistance even as she is penetrated reveals the character's persistence and durability. But if the framing of the sequence (frantic bongo music, farcical performance styles) disengages spectatorial identification, then the scene's representation of violence remains disturbing. For throughout, the criminal nature of the act is undermined: thus Paul (Santiago Lajusticia) is a half-witted escapee from prison, encouraged by his sister Juana, the lesbian maid, to tie her up and knock her unconscious (to simulate criminality) in order to cover up his future theft of Ramón's cameras. Moreover, the comically grotesque policemen are indistinguishable from the other narcissists and criminals in Almodóvar's rogues' gallery: one of them compares his dimple to that of Kirk Douglas; both are in the pay of video vamp Andrea. Similarly, Kika's complaints to Paul (that he should wear a condom when he rapes girls, that she can't wait all day for him to come) deny the specifically sexual nature of the act, implying that it is just another indignity forced upon her by an unknown man as unreasonable and intractable as her lovers Ramón and Nicholas.

It is not simply, then, that Almodóvar plays rape for laughs; it is that he follows Foucault's tendency, attacked by de Lauretis, of de-sexing rape, 'counter[ing] the technology of sex by breaking the bond between sexuality and crime' (p. 37). While it is clearly one of Almodóvar's aims (as it is for Foucault) to contest the operation of the state in the policing of 'perversion', de Lauretis argues that in cases such as this 'to release "bodies and pleasures" from the legal control of the state, and from the relations of power exercised through the technology of sex, is to affirm and perpetuate the present social relations which give men rights over women's bodies' (p. 37). Moreover, if Paul's parodic violence is offered as a paradigm of the supposed breakdown in social order (the epidemic of urban crime) to which Almodóvar claims his film is in part a response, for de Lauretis such violence is rather 'the sign of a "power struggle for the maintenance of a certain kind of social order"' (p. 34), one in which penetration is central to the representation of sex and the agent, gendered as male, must pass through the body of the woman (as boundary or obstacle) in order to advance the narrative. It thus follows that when the protagonist is female she must detach herself from identification with her own body, 'which she must come to perceive precisely as a space, the territory in which battle is waged' (p. 45). Like the women of New Guinea, encouraged by traditional, male doctors to identify as men in an incantation to facilitate childbirth, Kika in her travail alienates herself from her predicament, transforming herself into territory and con/fusing Paul's forced entry of her house and of her body: 'When I woke up he was already inside', she tells the bemused Ramón.

The problem, then, is that Kika, as a character, is both inside and outside her gender, an uncomfortable predicament which (as de Lauretis remarks) can be resolved or dispelled neither by desexualizing it (making rape just another imposition) nor by androgynizing it (making femininity a condition shared by characters of both sexes) (p. 11). For although we can argue that whatever the empirical gender of the actors' bodies, the gender of each character is produced by his or her position in the narrative (with Andrea masculinized as quest hero and Ramón feminized as passive victim of Nicholas), still gender sticks to Kika, in de Lauretis's suggestive image, 'like a wet silk dress' (p. 12). Almodóvar attempts to vindicate Kika's persistent and unnerving optimism, to 'theorize as positive the "relative" power of those oppressed by current social relations' (p. 17); but the action of the film suggests that her investment in femininity (in spontaneity and aestheticism) cannot pay off: it is 'a vested interest in the relative power (satisfaction, reward, payoff) which that [feminine] position promises (but does not necessarily fulfil)' (p. 16). Reconfirming femininity as the little space of relationships (scorning Ramón's male talk of 'Sadam and Sarajevo'), Kika cannot chart that 'passage from sociality to subjectivity, . . . or from cultural representations to self-representations' which is, for de Lauretis, 'a discontinuous passage' (p. 19).

One properly visual manifestation of that discontinuity is off-screen space. *Kika* appeals constantly and consistently to space-off: the cut from the set of Andrea's reality show to Juana's hypnotized stare at the TV screen reveals the look of the camera, normally naturalized; the repeated rising crane shots of Kika's building (a naked Ramón leaves bed alone; a bare-breasted Amparo seeks her bra before succumbing once more to Nicholas) compare and contrast the repressed ménage below with the ceaseless sexual traffic above. Space-off is sometimes signalled by an on-screen (intradiegetic) look: disappointed by Ramón's performance, Kika raises her eyes to the shaking chandelier, the sign of orgasmic union invisible to both character and audience. At others it remains extradiegetic: the camera tracks along the pavement outside the Círculo de Bellas Artes at night, to find Nicholas and Andrea framed inside by an illuminated window. Elsewhere it signals that genitality which poses the limit or boundary of representation in commercial cinema: Kika's unseen vagina, in which Paul moistens orange segments; Paul's ejaculating penis, whose semen splashes Andrea's face as she looks up at him from below.[23]

Just as woman moves 'back and forth across the boundaries of sexual difference' (with Kika alternately confirming and denying the gendered technology of sex), so space-off marks a 'movement from the . . . image produced by representation in a discursive or visual field to the space . . . not represented yet implied (unseen) in [images]', with the camera both dwelling on spectacular visual properties and appealing to unrepresentable sexual or subjective pleasures (pp. 25–6). However, this structural equation of gender and visual technology is not continuous:

> The movement in and out of gender as ideological representation . . . is a movement back and forth between the representation of gender . . . and what representation leaves out or . . . makes unrepresentable. . . . These two kinds of spaces are [not] in opposition . . . but exist concurrently and in contradiction. (p. 26)

Separate and heteronymous, woman and Woman, on-screen and off-screen, stage a border war or boundary breakdown which structurally determines the discontinuity of Almodóvar's narrative. That war is articulated by the competing demands made on the plot and the audience by the twin characters Kika and Andrea. It is no accident that while Kika lays claim to text (appropriating the name of the film and the bulk of its wordy dialogue) Andrea controls the field of the image (of costume and publicity shot). What I will suggest, then, is that if in Kika gender is technologized, with the 'essential' woman dissolved into visual paraphernalia (false eyelashes and fun fur), then in Andrea technology is gendered, with the 'indifferent' penetration of the vision machine (of video apparatus) revealed to be not simply instrumental to but rather complicit with the powers of patriarchy, even as it is embodied in a figure empirically gendered feminine.

But Andrea is less a woman than a cyborg, defined by Donna Haraway as a 'hybrid of machine and organism'. Haraway proposes the cyborg, ironically, as a 'matter of fiction and lived experiences that changes what counts as women's experience in the late twentieth century' (p. 149). The cyborg takes pleasure in the confusion of boundaries, just as Andrea embodies the conversion of flesh into technology (breasts, eyes and ears into arc lights, cameras and microphones) and just as she celebrates the blurring of the division between private and public (with intimate details splashed across the screen and the domestic TV room transformed into a market place). Discreet and dull when out of robotic uniform, Andrea also illustrates Haraway's paradox that 'our machines are disturbingly lively, and we ourselves frighteningly inert' (p. 152). Moreover, for Haraway there is a structural connection between 'bodily boundaries and social order' (p. 173): 'it is no accident that the symbolic system of the family of man – and so the essence of woman – breaks up at the same moment that networks of connection among people . . . are unprecedentedly multiple, pregnant, and complex' (p. 160). The end of woman (the violation of Kika) is thus concurrent with the rise of a technology of visualization whose social effects include the atomization and extreme commodification of (feminine) affect which *Kika*'s recreation of the reality show seeks, vainly, to parody.

For Haraway, however, there is no turning back: in the 'integrated circuit' of the 'informatics of domination' it is vain to call for a return to unitary identity based, as in Marxism, on 'labour as an ontological category' or, as in radical feminism, on sexual appropriation as the essence of woman (p. 159). While progressive politics has appealed to 'deepened dualisms . . . of idealism and materialism' supposedly effected by scientific culture and has 'recalled us to an imagined organic body to integrate our resistance', Haraway herself recommends a 'perverse shift of perspective' (p. 154) which welcomes the irony, simulation and biotic components of the cyborg. Now the 'world has been restructured through the social relations of science and technology' (p. 165), dualisms have lost their hold.

How does this paradoxical dynamic relate to Almodóvar's vision of the technocratic metropolis? *Kika*'s overt narrative attempts in vain to shore up boundaries and reinforce damaged and permeable membranes: the violation of Kika's intimacy by Andrea is unequivocally condemned; Kika's organicity (her 'feminine' sun dresses and soft, rounded body) is clearly contrasted with Andrea's hard and steely prostheses. However, within the film itself, Kika's naiveté and optimism do not stand as a form of resistance to the terror of technology, for Almodóvar cannot bring himself wholeheartedly to embrace nature even as he inveighs against the ravages of unnatural exploitation. It may be, then, that women's bodies are 'newly permeable to visualization and intervention', to the 'predatory nature of the photographic consciousness' (p. 169); but even Kika herself seems to hold an instrumental view of sexuality, treating her body as 'a kind of private satisfaction . . . machine', imperturbably turning to Nicholas when Ramón fails to satisfy her needs in bed.

But if there is no stable ground for resistance in the integrated circuit (no ideal untainted by material exploitation), then the moral (of cyborg politics, of *Kika*) may not be as depressing as at first appears. For just as the monstrous Andrea displaces the bland Kika, who is the nominal protagonist of the film, so the displacement of the old dualities may bring pleasures as well as problems for women. Haraway notes the implications of narrative here: 'Every story that begins with original innocence and privileges the return to wholeness imagines the drama of life to be individuation, separation, the birth of the self'. She proposes, with the cyborg, a new narrative, no longer reproductive, which 'does not pass through Woman' (p. 177): 'A cyborg body is not innocent; it was not born in a garden; it does not seek unitary identity and so generate antagonistic dualisms without end . . . ; it takes irony for granted' (p. 180).

After Kika's rape Almodóvar cuts from the pale disc of the moon to the revolving drum of the washing machine, which is cleaning the clothes in which she was violated. The graphic match between the two shots is not simply an elegant visual rhyme: it suggests that that equation of the ideal and the material which ran through the body of the woman can no longer be upheld, just as Kika's innocence and optimism cannot be sustained throughout the film. Kika ends by taking up with a new male lover, in a renewed investment in 'relative' power that fails to investigate the terms of the heterosexual contract which underwrites it. Andrea is punished by death for her boundary war (blood stains smearing her hi-tech armour), and not before she has been reduced to tearful femininity at the sight of the dying Nicholas. But just as Almodóvar's women cross the gender border and his camera hovers between space on and off screen, so his narrative hesitates between innocence and experience, the aesthetic and organic depth of the body and the ironic and strategic surface of the cyborg. It is an uncomfortable and unresolved position, at once inside and outside, which Almodóvar himself adopts in the publicity process: sometimes (as in *El País*) posing in the costumes of his characters; sometimes (as in the pressbook)[24] looming above those same characters who are now reduced to live chess pieces moved by the master. Identification and alienation, discontinuously and concurrently: such is the fate of *Kika*'s heroine, its creator and the audience.

Kika was criticized in Spain and abroad for 'unevenness' and 'discontinuity'; in the case of conservative critics, such as Angel Fernández Santos of *El País*, the complaint is explicitly nostalgic for classical narrative and its totalizing perspective.[25] As we have seen, both de Lauretis and Haraway attack the implications for women of this traditional plotting, with its appeal to nature as origin, to divisive dualisms and to a technology of gender which is far from innocent.

Ironically, however, *Kika* is both the effect and the instrument of changes in social relations in Spain associated with developments in visual technologies. For the dissolution of a once monolithic state broadcasting system and the rise of independent commercial TV channels in the late 1980s were accompanied by the progressive withdrawal of state support for cinema, which was left newly dependent on television (often foreign-owned) and on international coproducers.[26] The fractures and flows of Haraway's cyborg society are clearly visible in the Spain of the 1990s, with its massive structural unemployment, 'feminization' of labour and fracturing of the nation state, caught between the conflicting demands of the autonomous regions and the European Union.[27] The *Kika* that castigates the decline of Spain's media as symptomatic of social malaise is also the *Kika* that is co-funded by a French production company and was pre-sold, along with the vast bulk of 'Spanish' film production, to Canal +, a private TV channel, also partly French-owned.

Wary of such border wars, the film establishment granted *Kika* only one Goya (Spanish Oscar) at the awards ceremony for films released in 1993. In a nostalgic tribute to a satirist of Francoism, whose black humour is held to be typically Spanish, the Best Picture went to veteran Berlanga's disappointing *Todos a la cárcel* (Everyone Go to Jail). Fearful of fracture, the Academy, like the critics, rejected *Kika*, with its discontinuities and its flatness. But if the death or decline of Spanish cinema is visible both in *Kika* itself and in the ferocity with which its vision of the future was received in Spain, then this does not mean that we (that Spain) should simply embrace past masters. Rather, by gendering technology and technologizing gender Almodóvar has shown us that the vision machine is not indifferent and that Virilio's passage from dialectic to paradox may also be the shift from Woman to women (to a space-off unrepresented but inferred) no longer recontained or sealed into the image by the dead hand of classical narrativization. If Almodóvar, like Haraway, would 'rather be a cyborg than a goddess'[28] it is because he knows that, ironically and perversely, the new technologies of visualization hold possibilities of pleasure denied us by the *ancien régime* of the cinematic apparatus, even as those technologies enact ever more thoroughly, ever more efficiently, the 'more light' of Revolutionary terror.

NOTES

1   *El País Semanal*, Madrid (19 October 1993).

2   *Out*, New York (May 1994).

3   *Observer*, London (5 June 1994).

4   See my *Desire Unlimited: The Cinema of Pedro Almodóvar* (London: Verso, 1994).

5   For a lavishly illustrated tribute to and record of the *españolada* see Terenci Moix, *Suspiros de España: la copla y el cine de nuestro recuerdo* (Barcelona: Plaza y Janés, 1993). Camp icons from Concha Piquer to Concha Velasco are shown here in polka-dotted frocks.

6   For a recent critical account of homosexuality as identification with the opposite sex see Mandy Merck, 'The Train of Thought in Freud's "Case of Homosexuality in a Woman"', in the same author's collection of essays *Perversions: Deviant Readings* (London: Virago, 1993), pp. 13–32.

7   The quote is, of course, from Billy Wilder's *Sunset Boulevard* (1950). Compare the ironic caption to a cover shot of a wide-eyed and open-mouthed Almodóvar in the British gay glossy *Attitude* (July 1994): 'Outrageous!' In spite of Almodóvar's continuing disavowal of a gay

audience for his films, *Kika* benefited from copious and favourable coverage in the UK gay press.

8 This is my first citation from Paul Virilio, *The Vision Machine* (London: BFI, 1994); French original, *La Machine de vision* (Paris: Galilée, 1988). Virilio is known above all as the theorist of the reciprocal relation between reproductive technologies and war; see *War and Cinema: The Logistics of Perception* (London: Verso, 1989; French original, 1984).

9 To cite the press release (Mark Borkowski, 9 June 1994): 'On Thursday June 30th at 8.00 pm the coolest of London's hot-spots The Fridge plays host to superstyle stars of fashion and film in a night of fund-raising for Europe's leading HIV and AIDS centre, London Lighthouse.' This was the first time that Almodóvar had attempted to reproduce in London the lavish parties created in Madrid for the openings of his films.

10 'Future Chic', *Sight and Sound* (January 1994), pp. 6–10.

11 Rarely credited with any serious concerns in Spain, Almodóvar is regularly attributed intellectual ambitions in France; see Frédéric Strauss's location report 'The Almodóvar Picture Show', *Cahiers du Cinéma* 471 (September 1993), pp. 34–42; and the same author's interview with the director on *Kika* in *Pedro Almodovar* [sic]: *conversations avec Frédéric Strauss* (Paris: Cahiers du Cinéma, 1994), pp. 124–48. Strauss reproduces collages and draft designs by Dis Berlín which confirm the fusion of the organic (flowers, animals, women's bodies) and the technological (cameras, pylons, monitors) typical of the metropolitan vision machine.

12 Mayo was assistant cameraman on Almodóvar's *Mujeres al borde* (Women on the Verge, 1988) and principal cinematographer on *Tacones lejanos* (High Heels, 1991). For full details of his career see Francisco Llinás, *Directores de fotografía del cine español* (Madrid: Filmoteca Española, 1989), pp. 462–3.

13 The most influential, and most hostile, is Angel Fernández Santos in *El País* (6 November 1993). The title of his review ('La ley del desastre') recalls the title of his earlier review of *La ley del deseo* (The Law of Desire, 1987: 'La ley del exceso'), ironically so, given that one of his chief complaints against *Kika* is its supposed sterile repetition and self-citation. Once more, French critics vindicate terms taken to be negative by Spaniards, who remain faithful to the ideal of a 'well-made script': Strauss (*Pedro Almodovar*, p. 125) praises the apparent 'incoherence' of the plot, which he takes to be a freedom from the dictates of narrative convention.

14 This is the position of a sympathetic British critic such as Jonathan Romney: 'Time to Strike Camp', *New Statesman and Society* (1 July 1994).

15 The internal citation here is from Husserl, *L'Origine de la géométrie*.

16 Teresa de Lauretis, *Technologies of Gender: Essays on Theory, Film, and Fiction* (London: Macmillan, 1987).

17 Donna J. Haraway, *Simians, Cyborgs, and Women: The Reinvention of Nature* (London: Free Association, 1991).

18 For a more sophisticated version of this topos see Strauss's suggestion

(*Pedro Almodovar*, p. 148) that Kika 'both active and passive, organising the round dance of the characters and caught up herself in that movement, capable of giving life back [to Ramón] seems to be a metaphor for the role, the place, and the powers of the director'. Inversely, the figure of Almodóvar has often served as a screen for the projections of critics, most transparently in a recent Spanish monograph on the director whose last twenty pages are devoted to mediocre art works by the critic, who claims they were inspired by Almodóvar's cinema; Antonio Holguín, 'Apéndice gráfico', in *Pedro Almodóvar* (Madrid: Cátedra, 1994), pp. 347–66. Holguín's collages are also scattered amongst the text of his book.

19 'Fellini's Nine and a Half ', *Technologies of Gender*, pp. 95–106.

20 'The Violence of Rhetoric: Considerations on Representation and Gender', *Technologies of Gender*, p. 32.

21 Reproduced in *El País Semanal* (19 October 1993).

22 'The Technology of Gender', *Technologies of Gender*, p. 10.

23 In an unpublished paper read at the Deutscher Hispanistentag in Bonn (March 1995), Bernhard Teuber compares Andrea to the wounded Virgin of the Macarena, arguing that such 'perverse' sequences represent not so much a simple pleasure in profanity as an attempt to sacralize the flesh even as it is bathed in bodily fluids: 'Cuerpos sagrados: en torno a las imágenes perversas de la carne en España'.

24 *Kika: un film de Almodóvar* (Madrid: El Deseo S.A., 1993).

25 Even a sympathetic British critic such as Ricky Morgan laments the discontinuity of *Kika*'s narrative, echoing Spanish sentiments and citing 'a poorly crafted and fragmented plot which abandons characters and narrative threads mid-stream'; review in *Sight and Sound* (July 1994), p. 48.

26 The most detailed account of the contradictory state of the Spanish film industry at the time *Kika* was made is to be found in the five special issues of the trade journal *Moving Pictures* printed for the San Sebastián festival in September 1993. My thanks to Benedict Carver for providing me with copies of these issues. See also Carver's 'A Cheerful Recession', *Sight and Sound* (January 1994), p. 10, which stresses the rise of private funding to fill the gap left by the decline of state subsidy. For a reliable overview of Spanish media since the death of Franco see John Hooper, *The New Spaniards* (London: Penguin, 1995), pp. 306–41.

27 I treat the questions of nationality and the fragmentation of the family in the fifth chapter of this book.

28 *Simians*, p. 181.

PART II

Cuban Homosexualities

3

NÉSTOR ALMENDROS/

REINALDO ARENAS:

Documentary, Autobiography and Cinematography

1. FROM THE REAL TO THE VISIBLE

Exile, homosexuality, an early death from the effects of AIDS: it is not the similarities between Néstor Almendros and Reinaldo Arenas that are initially apparent, but rather the differences between them. Barcelona-born cinematographer and critic Almendros left his adopted homeland of Cuba in 1962, just three years after Castro entered Havana; the autobiography he first published in French in 1980 is rigorously restricted to his professional life, the very model of discretion. Novelist and poet Arenas, on the other hand, left his native Cuba only in 1980 with the *Mariel* exodus, after suffering many years of harsh repression; and his autobiography of 1992 is scandalously indiscreet, extravagantly confessional. The respective titles of these autobiographies are symptomatic. Almendros's *Días de una cámara* (literally 'days of a camera', translated as *Man with a Camera*)[1] characteristically effaces the writer's subjectivity, fuses him with his professional instrument. Arenas's *Antes que anochezca*[2] (Before Night Falls), on the other hand, invites the reader to share the urgency of the scenes of its writing: first in Havana's Lenin Park where the author, a fugitive from the Castroist security forces, could write only by daylight before night fell; and later in exile in New York, where he struggled to rewrite the manuscript when facing the definitive darkness of death. There is a photograph reproduced in *Antes que anochezca* which might also be read as emblematic: seated on a sofa with mutual friends at a private house in Spain, Arenas gestures vividly to unseen spectators outside the frame; Almendros looks down, apparently immersed in reading an exile newspaper. Extravagance and reticence, these are the overt messages of both text and picture.

Both Almendros and Arenas left complimentary references to each other's work in their respective oeuvres. But where they most clearly coincided was in Arenas's participation in the feature Almendros co-directed with fellow exile Orlando Jiménez Leal, the documentary *Mauvaise conduite* (Improper Conduct, 1984) (Plate 8). A decade has now passed since the film's then unprecedented indictment of revolutionary Cuba's homophobia. And it is possible to look back at the polemic the film provoked and to reread that polemic in the context of the two autobiographies.

The questions raised by *Mauvaise conduite* are more fundamental than they at first appeared; and they are posed all the more urgently now that the eclipse of Marxism as a political and theoretical force has rendered the articulation of new forms of resistance a priority. Those questions are drawn from the three broad areas of representation, nationality and identity. First, *Mauvaise conduite* offers itself, like Arenas's subsequent autobiography, as pure transparency, with film simply a vehicle for the imaging of truth. Almendros spoke at the time of the film's release of his wish to include all the testimony spoken by the witnesses without editing of any kind; and the two-hour final cut was edited down from an eight-hour version which Almendros considered to be the 'true' film. Shot full face, often in tight close-up, and illuminated for the most part by available light sources, the film's twenty-eight witnesses speak as if directly to the spectator, without interference from the cinematic mechanism. But, of course, film is not or not only ontology, the representation of subjects and objects which precede it; it is also language, a complex means of representation serving actively to construct those subjects and objects. As we shall see, *Mauvaise conduite* was criticized on its release for precisely this theoretical naiveté, for its apparent faith in the unmediated presence of truth in art. The problem remains: How can we reconcile this scepticism towards artistic truth, so commonplace in cultural studies since the seventies, with the respect due to the testimony of the survivors of state terror? Or, to put it more bluntly, how did the critique of representation become an apology for dictatorship?

This leads on to the second question, that of nationality. There seems little doubt that the Castro regime's treatment of homosexuals has proved to be a unique point of contention both on the island and amongst supporters and detractors abroad. Given the prevalence of homophobia throughout Latin America and elsewhere, it is by no means inevitable that this should have been the case. Why is it that homosexuality has been such a sensitive issue in and for Cuba? And how did foreign responses vary according to the nationality of the spectator? As we shall see, Anglo-American readings of the film differed sharply from those of French critics, more sympathetic perhaps to Latin American homosexualities than English-speakers, whether gay or straight; and it seems likely that any answer will have both a historical and a psychic dimension.

Here we come to the third question, that of identity. Neither in *Mauvaise conduite* nor in the two autobiographies do we find gay identities of a kind familiar to US or UK spectators. One British critic complained that only two of the film's speaking heads identified as gay on screen, and they were readily identifiable queens, whose 'improper conduct' was already flagrantly visible. But to criticize the reticence of Almendros's autobiography and his witnesses on film may be simply to impose foreign norms on differing forms of subjectivity. What are those forms and how are they rendered visible to us?

One publicity shot for *Mauvaise conduite* shows Arenas calmly seated on a chair, illuminated by a window to the right. A French film magazine ran this picture with the caption 'La lumière naturelle'.[3] The caption might seem to reconfirm that 'natural' simplicity shared by both Almendros and Arenas in their faith in personal testimony. However, Almendros's career as a cinematographer in Europe and the US reveals that 'natural light' is not as simple to achieve as might at first appear. And I shall argue that far from being naive, as has often been supposed, both Almendros and Arenas share in their artistic practice a healthy awareness of the limits of representation and of identity, of the necessary collusion between fiction and the real. If truth, light and life are inextricable in what Derrida once called the 'white mythology', then Cuba stands as a twilight zone in which contraries merge and fuse or, in Freud's resonant phrase, are 'reversed into their opposites'. In contrast to this crazy 'up and down dream' of the Castristas is Almendros's and Arenas's vision of the beach: the erotic location par excellence in which anonymous bodies are set in motion, silhouetted against the water, against the light.

Let us look more closely at *Mauvaise conduite* itself and its detractors' objections to it, before moving on to the autobiographies. As Almendros himself explained after a screening of his film at New York University in 1984,[4] the two hours of screen time are structured according to a three-part movement: the first part has 'innocent testimonies' offered by non-intellectual witnesses such as Caracol, a gloriously extravagant Afro-Cuban queen; the second part has intellectuals (Guillermo Cabrera Infante, Juan Goytisolo, Susan Sontag) reflecting on that testimony; the third part is the testimony of those who had 'the most terrible experiences', such as Armando Valladares (imprisoned for twenty-two years) (Plate 9) and René Ariza (condemned to eight years in prison because his writings were judged to attack Castro and 'lack literary value'), with whom the film ends. This structural movement (from testimony to reflection and back to testimony) is complemented by a chronological narrative: the first part treats the notorious UMAP camps of the 1960s (motto: Work Will Make You Men), in which gays were condemned to forced labour; the second the impact of new laws on 'extravagance' and 'dangerousness' in the 1970s; the third the *Mariel* exodus and its consequences in the 1980s. Almendros notes that the editing is as 'unadorned' as possible, leaving jump cuts where material has been omitted; that the *mise-en-scène* is equally minimalist ('the less . . . the better'); and that, most unusually for a film by a cinematographer, sound takes precedence over image, the spoken word over visuals. There is no background music to detract from the testimony; and the only distractions from Arenas and Jiménez Leal's original footage (shot of necessity outside Cuba) are archive shots of the revolutionaries' entry into Havana, of Cuban crowds dutifully demonstrating against the 'vermin' of the *Mariel*, and of Castro himself vigorously denying the existence of repression in Cuba.

Almendros laments that he was unable for financial reasons to shoot in 35 mm because the latter 'is closer to reality than [the] 16 mm' he was obliged to use in *Mauvaise conduite*; and he claims that 'faces [are] shown frontally, because in profile one sees only half of the truth of the face'. With witnesses' eyelines adjusted as far as possible to the lens, 'the audience . . . feel[s] that the people being interviewed were almost talking to them'. Such statements are clearly a gift to those critics who believe that, on the contrary, film is by no means innocent and 'reality' is called into being by those media which claim, simply, to reflect it. Ironically, however, those same critics who marshalled the sceptical arsenal of critical theory against Almendros's modest documentary give evidence elsewhere of a credulity towards Castroism that can only be called theological. Typical here is the review in the then left-leaning London listings magazine *City Limits*, which both encourages its readers to 'get out their critical scalpels' for a film that 'promises to tell the whole Truth' and suggests that to criticize Cuba at all is to play into the hands of the US imperialist enemy.[5]

Let us look at two influential critics in the US and the UK. B. Ruby Rich's piece in *American Film*,[6] run under the unfortunate title 'Bay of Pix', attacks *Mauvaise conduite*'s use of talking heads, claiming that by editing out the historical and social context of such testimonies the film becomes 'fiction, not documentary':

> The film is so determined to ignore the advances in standard of living, education, health, and access to culture that it is crucial to remember what is omitted. In place of history, the film offers myth. In place of data or documented sources, there is only first-person testimony. In place of understanding, only shock. *Improper Conduct* cynically uses homosexuality as a wedge to splinter what little sympathy for Cuba remains among American intellectuals. (p. 59)

Here, we are far from Almendros's faith in the revelation of truth, caught full face in natural light. And Rich's sceptical attention to the power of montage (its capacity to create meaning through omission as well as selection or combination) would have to be taken seriously, if the film had indeed failed to address the historical context she erroneously claims it neglects.[7] Elsewhere, however, Rich promises *American Film*'s readers the 'true story of homosexuality in Cuba' and the 'real story behind the film's making'. Sceptical epistemology would thus seem to have its limits. And there is throughout the piece an appeal to a rhetoric of reversal which is curiously emphatic: thus 'the stories ring true in inverse proportion to the viewer's familiarity with Cuba' (p. 58); or again 'only ignorance regarding the anti-Castro émigré network could cause audiences to accept this film as a defence of homosexuality, when the issue is simply being used as a sort of intellectuals' MX missile, aimed not at Christopher Street, but at Havana' (p. 59).[8] In the twilight zone of Cuban polemic, geographic and epistemological positions are reversed, with New York changing places with Havana, and the revelations offered by the film condemned as the obscurity of propaganda.

Another critic who makes quite explicit his identification with the 'Socialist ideals' of Cuba is Briton Michael Chanan, author of an exhaustively documented history of Cuban cinema. Chanan's *The Cuban Image*[9] opens with an attack on *Mauvaise conduite*, then recently released (he was also prominent in attacking Almendros when the latter presented his film at the London Film Festival). In Chanan, as in Rich, but more explicitly, the critique of representation fuses with an overt political commitment which leads its author into sophistries based once more on a rhetoric of reversal. Thus Chanan's introduction claims that 'film is an incomparable means, in the right hands, with which to show the way things are (whatever the theoretical status you ascribe to the image in its quality as a sign)' (p. 2). Struggling to reconcile film as ontology ('to show the way things are') with film as language ('the theoretical status of the sign') Chanan is forced to appeal to the external legitimation of political control ('in the right hands'). There is no doubt for Chanan that those hands are not Almendros's. Dismissing *Mauvaise conduite* as 'tactical propaganda' ('a theory and a concept which go back to the Nazis') (p. 5), Chanan attacks the film for its 'relentless disregard for dialectical argument, [lack of] exploration of the contradictions [the interviews] pose, or respect for the viewer's powers of discrimination' (p. 5). 'In the end', he writes, 'one has to doubt whether all of these stories can be true.' On the one hand, then, Chanan claims that in his own case no 'apologia is required for showing commitment', 'no apology' needed for writing a 'partisan history' (pp. 4, 6); on the other hand, he attacks Almendros for failing to observe those theoretical fetishes (dialectic, contradiction) beloved of Marxist cultural critics, and for making his own political commitment embarrassingly clear.

In a curious variation of the 'things are getting better' argument offered by many apologists for Castro, Chanan blames revolutionary homophobia on the supposed successes of Cuban feminism:

> [The repression of gays] seems to me . . . the result of the advancement of women within the Revolution. . . . Especially in a society as

intensely machista as Cuba, the advancement of women represents a threat to men, or to a certain kind of man, and men whose own sexuality is thus threatened are all too liable to start taking it out on other men. (p. 6)

For Chanan, the focus of identification thus shifts from gay men, the victims of surveillance, imprisonment and exile, to their heterosexual tormenters, stricken by an identity crisis which can safely be blamed on overassertive women.

Hence in this rhetoric of reversal marshalled by apologists for dictatorship, bottom becomes top, knowledge ignorance, and light dark. Oppressed and powerless lesbians and gays are dismissed as the unwitting (or sometimes witting) instruments of an omnipotent oppressor, the United States. The knowledge of oppression exiles bring with them is branded as ignorance of the Revolution's true motives and effects, which, in the final instance, must be in the interests of all Cuba's unwilling citizens. Finally, the enlightenment of witnesses' testimony (to themselves, to others) is transformed into a cloud of false consciousness, the obscurity of a subjectivism wholly untheorized and nondialectical. At best such witnesses are stigmatized as ingenuous fools who know not what they say; at worst, they are culpable criminals, aiming cinematic missiles at the ever-vulnerable revolutionary citadel.

Chanan's account of the Cuban film industry in the early years of Castroism coincides in outline with Almendros's, in the brief version in his autobiography; but it also offers further evidence of the uneasy coalition between leftist politics and critical theory in the 1980s. The emergence of an independent Cuban film sector after the Revolution was preceded by the aficionado movement of the 1940s and 1950s which itself focused on the first cine-club in the country, set up by Almendros and Guillermo Cabrera Infante, amongst others.[10] With the arrival of the long-haired revolutionaries (much admired by Arenas) in 1959 and the setting up of ICAIC, the national film institute, the stage was set for production of documentary and subsequently full-length features in a national and more latterly Socialist vein. Directors such as Tomás Gutiérrez Alea were to win Cuba much-coveted film prizes from abroad. Dissension was immediate, however. Almendros's own short documentary on beach life, *Gente en la playa* (People on the Beach), filmed informally and mainly with a

hidden camera, was confiscated and had to be edited clandes-
tinely. The autobiography reproduces a tantalizing still: bodies
silhouetted against a burnt-out background, the blinding light
of the tropical sun reflected on the ocean. A more celebrated
short called *P.M.*, directed by Saba Cabrera Infante and *Mauvaise
conduite*'s Orlando Jiménez Leal, was also banned. Now dismissed
from ICAIC, Almendros gave *P.M.* a favourable review in his
role as critic for the magazine *Bohemia*.[11] The ensuing conflict
culminated in Castro's much-debated 1961 speech 'Words to the
Intellectuals' and in the closing down of *Lunes de Revolución*,
the cultural supplement edited by Guillermo Cabrera Infante. In
Chanan's version of this polemic the banning of *P.M.* can no
longer be called 'the Revolution's first act of censorship'. Rather,
he argues, 'it is more enlightening to see [the controversy] as the
dénouement of the incipient conflict between different political
trends which lay beneath the surface during the period of the
aficionado movement in the 50s' (p. 105). Just as previously
the manifest injustice of the regime's treatment of homosexuals
was deflected on to the supposed latent identity crisis of its
heterosexual men, so here a conspicuous act of repression is
transmuted into the imperceptible stirrings of hidden cultural
conflict.

But what interests me here is not Chanan's servility (he faith-
fully transcribes each interruption for 'applause' in Castro's
speech); nor his sophistry (he cites official sources claiming that
the closing of *Lunes* 'established better conditions for different
artistic tendencies to engage with each other on more equal
terms'); it is rather his appeal to film theory to justify state censorship. Thus *P.M.*'s depiction in free cinema style of the mainly
black, working-class bars of the waterfront was intolerable not
because of its lack of uplifting revolutionary moral, but because
its 'irresponsibility' was aesthetic as well as political:

> They had begun to sense at ICAIC that the camera was not the
> unproblematic kind of instrument the apologists for *P.M.*
> supposed. It does not – to paraphrase the French film theorist
> Serge Daney – involve a single straight line from the real to the
> visible and thence to its reproduction on film, in which a simple
> truth is faithfully reflected. . . . Daney says 'in a world where "I see"
> is automatically said for "I understand" such a fantasy has probably
> not come about by chance. The dominant ideology which equates

the real with the visible has every interest in encouraging it.'
At ICAIC they were beginning to perceive that revolutionary
change required a rupture with this equation, which meant among
other things being constantly on guard against received aesthetic
formulae. (p. 103)

It is an unfortunate irony, unmentioned by Chanan, that one
reason for Almendros's flight from Cuba was his realization that
he was unable to make those revolutionary changes in lighting
that were to win him such fame as a cinematographer abroad.
For Cuban cinema still clung to received aesthetic formulae even
as it proclaimed its definitive rupture with the political past. But
of course the point Chanan borrows from Daney is not technical,
but theoretical: it is only by challenging the white mythology that
collapses light, visibility and truth that the cinematic apparatus
can be denaturalized and the actual relations between spectator,
cinema and society be rendered intelligible. But if the equation
between sight and understanding is a fantasy promoted by the
dominant (capitalist) ideology, then visibility is itself placed under
suspicion. It must be interrogated for its unspoken compliance
with a spectatorial regime as pervasive as it is insidious.

Here then is the theoretical justification for dismissing the
testimony provided by *Mauvaise conduite*'s witnesses: it is their
very visibility (full-face close-ups, flooded with natural light) that
is unforgivable, that renders them complicit with the regime of
political and aesthetic norms fostered by international capitalism.
But this theoretical question is also national. For in Cuba also
and much more immediately, the trial of visibility was enforced as
a criterion for measuring the degree of 'social pathology' exhibited
by gay men. Thus the declaration of the First National Congress on
Education and Culture of 1971 stressed the need to 'differentiate
between cases' and establish their relative 'degree of degradation'.[12] Proposing preventative measures such as the 'extension
of the coeducational system' and the prohibition of 'known homosexuals' influencing 'the development of our young people', the
declaration also dealt with 'fashions, customs, and extravagant
behaviour', asserting 'the necessity of maintaining the monolithic
and ideological unity of our people . . . [through] direct confrontation in order to bring about the elimination of extravagant
aberrations' (p. 180). Ironically, then, the Cuban witnesses whose
testimonies were discounted by foreign intellectuals from the safety

of New York and London ('finally we must ask if all these stories can be true') had already suffered a more rigorous trial of visibility in which their appearance had been scrutinized for its divergence from pre-set ideological norms.

All too visible for Anglo-American critics, the very transparency of their testimony rendering them suspect to theoretical eyes and ears, still Almendros's speakers were not yet visible enough. Why, foreigners asked, did so few of them (Arenas included) fail to identify themselves as lesbian or gay? Jane Root wrote in the London *Monthly Film Bulletin* that *Mauvaise conduite* was 'both an attack on and a betrayal of the relaxed, self-affirming warmth generated by gay films in the *Word is Out/Harvey Milk* tradition'.[13] More sympathetic critics might consider that those who had been persecuted for their excessive visibility had some reason to be circumspect even in exile; and that Cuban refugees should not be expected to make obeisance to North American documentary styles. Indeed Arenas's autobiography is, as we shall see, scathing in its dismissal of an American gay lifestyle it sees as anything but 'relaxed' and 'warm'. Moreover, if we look at French responses to the film, which were much more favourable than those in the US and the UK,[14] we find possible answers to both the question of nationality (Why is homosexuality so important for Cuba?) and that of identity (Why do Cuban lesbians and gays appear so reluctant to 'affirm' themselves?).

Michel Celemenski in *Cinématographe*[15] claims that 'the uprooting [*extirpation*] of homosexuality has a vital role in the erection of socialism' (p. 27). Most telling for him is not the brutality with which laws of 'extravagant behaviour' and 'improper conduct' are enforced, but rather the ideological implications of 'reeducation'. While the Nazi appeal to work (Arbeit macht frei) was merely cynical, one of the lies intended to ensure the docility of death-camp victims, the Communist belief in the salutary value of labour (Work Will Make You Men) is naively proclaimed as a scientific truth. This supernatural status of work, at the heart of Marxist folklore, makes it available to the authorities as a form of shock treatment, to be administered with Ubu-esque zeal. Communist puritanism and terror are thus derived from a tenacious attachment to metascience:

> Communism is a form of morality, and its structuration depends
> on the rigorous integration of all human functions and, a fortiori,

the function of love. Life is production, love reproduction. . . . The relegation by Marxism of secondary elements of alienation (such as the *condition* of women, the *question* of the Jews, the *problem* of nationality) is no mere tactical sideline of the Communist project. The teleological hypothesis of Marxism . . . bears witness to a universal mission seeking not to ensure the development of a future liberated . . . society, but rather to forge a uniform identity in the image of the industrial ideals from which [Communism] itself emerged and on whose behalf it acts in the Third World countries it has colonized. (my translation, p. 27)

The language would be familiar to those who framed the Cuban decree on 'extravagance', bent as they were on preserving the 'monolithic . . . unity of our people'. But if the homophobia of Cuba is deeply embedded in its Marxist ideology, then that same homophobia manifests itself in the most transparent ways: an attachment to appearance, whereby a readily visible homosexuality is thought to be more 'serious' a crime than the invisible, closeted variety; and a totalitarian system of surveillance which 'possesses the unique ability of rendering any gesture suspicious' (p. 28).

For French critics, then, better versed in theory than their English-speaking opposite numbers, the oppression of gays in Cuba is by no means accidental, but is rather structurally determined by the centrality of the labour theory of value to Marxist doctrine. And writing in *Cahiers du Cinéma*, Charles Tesson further suggests that the power of *Mauvaise conduite* lies in the fact that Cuba has made itself particularly vulnerable to attack by cinematic means: unable or unwilling to lay bare the contradictions of its own history on film, Cuba lays itself open to cinematic critique.[16] Like Celemenski, Tesson also stresses the way repression operates in the field of the visible; the body is interrogated for supposed external signs of inner vice: clothing, hairstyle, gesture and posture. This he calls a 'physical violation' which takes place 'in the intimacy of bodies and their representation' (p. 48). It is perhaps significant that Tesson begins his piece by referring to Almendros's early documentary *Gente en la playa* and claims that the love of natural light has been Cuba's continuing contribution to Almendros's distinguished career in Europe and the US.[17]

But if French critics prove more sensitive than English-speakers to both theoretical nuance and physical sensation (paying particular attention to the quality of light and sound in *Mauvaise conduite*), what is clearly lacking from their accounts is the sense of responsibility towards a lesbian and gay audience we find in British and North American reviewers. This absence is even more extreme in Spanish responses: trade journal *Cineinforme*, reporting that the film had won a major award, manages to avoid informing its readers of the nature of the oppression the film documents;[18] even Almendros speaks laconically in his autobiography of 'repression in Cuba'. However, what seems like closetry to English-speakers may have a different meaning in Latin cultures. And Anglo-American binaries would prove quite incapable of coping with the actual range of sexual preferences revealed outside the film by *Mauvaise conduite*'s talking heads: from Arenas's scorn of US gay male separatism to Goytisolo's limitation of his male sexual partners to Arabs who consider themselves heterosexual.

Unwilling as they are simply to assume the existence of a clearly delimited lesbian and gay community, Cubans, French and Spaniards are obliged to examine homophobia in the context of other forms of oppression and are unable to draw a neat dividing line between them. There is thus a final irony in the film's reception: while critics such as Chanan claimed that *Mauvaise conduite* allowed no space for the audience to exercise its own judgement, they also attacked the film at precisely that point where it chose not to specify and refused to direct its spectators. Deprived of explicit guidance as to the sexual identity of the participants, we are left suspended before faces bathed in light, tempted to retrace once more that trial of visibility to which some were subjected with such terrible consequences in Cuba.

2. NÉSTOR ALMENDROS: PROFESSIONAL OF LIGHT

François Truffaut's introduction to *Man with a Camera* notes that one aim of the cinematographer is 'to interpret the desire of a director who knows exactly what he does not want but can't explain what he does want' (p. viii). This modestly self-effacing role (of interpretation without direction) is confirmed by Almendros himself in his opening section, 'Some Thoughts on My Profession'. He writes: 'The director of photography . . . does everything and nothing . . . [He must] immerse himself in the director's manner. It is not "our" film, but "his" film' (pp. 3, 4). Tracing the history of

movie lighting from the mannered direct lighting of the 1940s to
the more subtle reflected lighting of the New Wave and after,
Almendros reclaims a narrative invisible to most cinemagoers,
and one which aspires to ever-increasing transparency and 'naturalness'. Thus Almendros scorns from the very beginning artificial
filters, gauzes and diffusers (p. 10) and is impatient with the clichéd
back lighting he was taught when studying in Rome, supposed
capital of Neorealism (p. 31). Experimenting with 'available light'
(that is, without artificial supplements) his first short was *58–59,* a
record of New Year's celebrations in Times Square in which people
are shown 'in silhouette against a luminous background' of neon
billboards and shop windows (p. 32). This clearly anticipated the
Cuban-made *Gente en la playa,* in which Almendros was confirmed
in his belief that 'natural light [was] more beautiful than artificial'
(p. 36).

Exiled by Castro (as he had been by Franco and Batista),
Almendros lent his skills to the deceptively simple projects
of New Wave directors in the 1960s. Thus his innovative use of
reflected light for interiors complements Eric Rohmer's severely
functional image and direct sound (p. 61); his 'justification' of
light sources on period sets (candles, lamps and bonfires) aids
Truffaut's meticulously 'calligraphic' reconstructions (p. 104); and
his discreet camerawork echoes Maurice Pialat's 'respect for
reality' (p. 119). But if Almendros's great innovation was the use of
documentary lighting for feature films, that naturalness was often
the result of meticulous and ingenious experiment. For example,
in Truffaut's *Adèle H.* (1974) the 'justified' lighting which appears
to come from period oil lamps was in fact derived from household
electric bulbs whose cords ran to batteries hidden under the
actors' clothes (p. 104). And Almendros approaches the recon-
struction of a period not through direct documentary evidence,
but rather with reference to a contemporary school of painting
(p. 102). Moreover, if Almendros loves to 'light by eye' and 'look
through the viewfinder [him]self', he is constantly aware of the
technical limits to filmic representation, writing: 'I need the frame
with . . . its limits . . . There is no artistic transposition without
limits . . . What counts in two dimensional art is not only what is
seen but what is not seen, what does not let itself be seen' (p. 12).
In his professional practice Almendros thus knows full well that
omission is as significant as inclusion, and that it is the invisible
which enables the visible to be seen.

Famous in France, Almendros was invited to work more frequently in the US in the 1970s. Most important was his contribution to Terence Malick's *Days of Heaven* (1976), for which he won an Academy Award. Once more, Almendros attempted an absolute simplicity: 'subtract[ing] technical aids ... to leave the image bare' (p. 171); using hand-operated heads for pan shots (instead of mechanical gears) so that 'the operator becomes all of a piece with the camera' (p. 175); and shooting 'characters silhouetted against the flames' of burning wheat fields in a *tour de force* of natural lighting (p. 180). *Days of Heaven* also led Almendros to heights of ingenuity: in outdoor scenes involving crosscut dialogue both actors were shot in the same spot with their backs to the sun. Cinematic continuity (the need for a background with the same luminous value) here led to what Almendros calls a 'flagrant contradiction in realist ethics' (p. 181). The reliance on natural light in extreme conditions forced Almendros to hold the lens stop wide open, leading to a minimal depth of field (p. 184). The preference for working 'in the camera', thus avoiding optical effects in the laboratory, led him to run film backwards so that locusts dropped from planes would appear to be rising out of the fields (p. 185). And Almendros's later work in the 1980s makes explicit this collusion between nature and artifice. 'Stylization' is, he notes, essential to convince the viewer of 'historical realism' (p. 220); the use of directional lighting in Truffaut's Occupation drama *Le dernier Métro* (1980) is 'ironic' (p. 251); in the final analysis, there can be no simple dividing line between naturalism, stylization and verisimilitude (p. 269).

What is striking, then, about Almendros's meticulous professional autobiography is that it shows how, just as he brought documentary lighting to features, so he brought feature techniques to documentary: the 'transparent' devices of *Mauvaise conduite*, most particularly the quest for a natural light justified within the frame itself, were ones Almendros had spent over twenty years perfecting. Significant here is the reference to Vermeer as an artistic precedent for light slanting through the window: Almendros uses it to describe both *Mauvaise conduite* and *Days of Heaven*. However to claim that Almendros was indeed, contrary to his critics, sceptically aware of the limits of representation and the language of film is not to invalidate the artistic and political project of *Mauvaise conduite*. Rather it is to endow that project with greater dignity and seriousness. For just as the limits of the frame throw the objects within it into luminous relief, so the limits of human mortality lend that professional and personal life a resonant pathos.

Almendros tells us that much of *Days of Heaven* was shot, at the director's insistence, at the brief 'magical hour' between sunset and nightfall:

> All day we would work to get the actors and the camera ready; as soon as the sun had set we had to shoot quickly, not losing a moment. For these few minutes the light is truly magical, because no one knows where it is coming from. The sun is not to be seen, but the sky can be bright, and the blue of the atmosphere undergoes strange mutations. . . . Each day, like Joshua in the Bible, Malick wanted to stop the sun in its imperturbable course so as to go on shooting. (p. 182)

That moment of radiance, all the more precious because of its brevity, is not only the truncated career of Almendros, professional of light; it is also Reinaldo Arenas's experience of desire and of writing, enjoyed all the more intensely because of the awareness that it takes place in the shadow of dictatorship and mortality.

3. REINALDO ARENAS:
THE TRIAL OF VISIBILITY

Reinaldo Arenas's persona, extravagant, humorous, spiteful, could hardly be further from Almendros's studied seriousness. Yet Arenas also appeals to a criterion of naturalness or authenticity which will have cultural critics reaching for their theoretical scalpels. Just as Almendros sought to draw a straight line from the real to the visible by flooding faces with natural light, so Arenas attempts (with scant regard for 'the theoretical status of the sign') to shed light on the darkness of Cuban dictatorship and speak the truth of his experience as a gay man, a dissident writer and a political prisoner. However, as in the case of Almendros once more, truth and nature will prove to be stubbornly indefinable, their stability undermined by the very homosexuality which Arenas insists on rendering gloriously, extravagantly visible. Moreover, Arenas's erotic and literary adventures are framed by the brief narrative of his AIDS-related illness, with which he begins his autobiography, and the unforgiving suicide note, with which he ends it. Like Almendros's 'magical' twilight hour, the truncated time span of *Antes que anochezca* is rendered all the more intense, all the more radiant, by its pathetic brevity.

Composed *in extremis* (dictated into a tape recorder and subsequently revised), *Antes que anochezca* aspires to the condition of a speaking voice: loquacious, undisciplined, shamelessly egocentric. This oral register is confirmed by Arenas's narration of his childhood, characterized by an unmediated closeness to nature: his first memory is of the excretion of a monstrous centipede, the product of his infantile habit of eating earth (p. 17). The trees of his provincial home hold a secret life to be 'deciphered' by the child who climbs them (p. 22); its flooded rivers offer the prospect of merger and annihilation (p. 36). Little Reinaldo is the fortunate possessor of a boundless, nonspecific eroticism, roused by animals and plants, by the bouncing of his buttocks on his uncle's swollen penis as they trek to town on horseback (p. 40). And as he grows to adulthood, by way of a desultory participation in the campaigns against Batista and a move to the longed-for capital, his innumerable erotic encounters come to stand as a 'territory of beauty' which challenges the 'anti-aesthetic' tedium of dictatorship (p. 113). It is an erotic rebellion typified by his frantic coupling with a naked recruit by the side of a highway, their bodies lit by the headlights of speeding vehicles (p. 118).

But the natural element of love is water. For the child, the sight of men bathing in the river, their genitals shining in the sun, had been a 'revelation' (p. 26); for the adult, the beach is the erotic location par excellence: in the huts of La Concha respectable married men give themselves up to fevered gay desires (p. 126); and Arenas's invaluable flippers even give him access to underwater intimacies (p. 127). The flashing of sun on sea, the brief mystery of the tropical sunset glimpsed while swimming (p. 136), these are not merely sensual but fully sexual pleasures.

A shamelessly explicit narrative of sex, *Antes que anochezca* is also and simultaneously a chronicle of writing which is equally obsessive and repetitive: Arenas will be condemned constantly to rewrite lost or confiscated manuscripts. Having procured a nominal post in the National Library, Arenas is free to pursue his literary education, aided by friendships with distinguished gay writers such as Virgilio Piñera. The bodily rhythm of writing is parallel to that of cruising the parks and beaches; and the regime's repressive vigilance makes unauthorized composition and conjugation equally taboo, equally hidden from sight. However, if sex and writing are authentic activities which tolerate no prohibition, they are also insidiously affected by the state censorship which would keep them under wraps. On Castro's entry into Havana in 1959, it is the splendid hair and beards of the revolutionaries that attract Arenas's amorous attention (p. 68); and the youth and labour camps of state Socialism are ideal breeding grounds for same-sex desire. On the paradise of the Isla de los Pinos, the 'erotic fury' of five thousand military recruits is in direct proportion to their Revolution-inspired repression (p. 119). And more than once Arenas hints that the transcendent importance of literature in Cuba derives in part from the regime's implacable policing of those who seek to practise it. If, as Almendros claims, there can be no artistic transposition without limits, then those limits are in Cuba flagrantly, brutally clear.

What Arenas prizes above all in sex is spontaneity and freedom from convention. This is why he suspends all sexual activity when incarcerated in Havana's notorious Morro prison on a trumped-up charge of corruption of minors. But on closer examination, the 'naturalness' of his homosexuality is shot through by cultural convention and role play. Thus Arenas gives a tragicomic categorization of 'four kinds of queens' in Cuba (pp. 103–4); and he defines himself as a *loca* who seeks his opposite: a 'real man' (p. 132). Lamenting from exile the tedious reciprocity of gay sex in the US, he eulogizes the objects of his love in Cuba: men with wives or girlfriends who enjoy penetrating other men. Just as such men cannot be defined by conventional binaries, so Cuban beaches or clubs are undivided along sexual lines (p. 133). Civil rights may be all very well for First World gays; but the US lifestyle Arenas encounters in exile is 'desolate'.

Ironically, it was this imprecision of definition that facilitated Arenas's inclusion in the *Mariel* exodus of 1980. Having been imprisoned for 'public scandal', Arenas presented himself to the authorities not as a dissident writer, but as a passive queer (the active variety was not considered to be homosexual and was therefore denied permission to leave) (p. 301). Asked to walk in front of a panel of psychologists, he had no trouble in persuading them which category he belonged to, in spite of the fact that the autobiography tells us with some relish of the times he enjoyed 'playing the man' in bed. Having passed this final trial of visibility, Arenas was to submit himself to what he would call the third tyranny he was to suffer: after Batista and Castro came the equally unforgiving US dollar.

One response to *Antes que anochezca* from inside Cuba expresses affectionate incredulity towards his gleefully hostile treatment of former friends;[19] we may indeed come to doubt whether all of Arenas's stories can be true. To dismiss the book as tactical propaganda against Castro would, however, be mistaken. Relentlessly obsessive in his concern for the body, Arenas barely attempts to take up that abstracted position from which truth is handed down to the believers. If this is a partisan history, it quite rightly makes no apology for its commitment. After dragging himself, mortally sick, to Miami Beach to await the end in his preferred location, Arenas is disappointed once more: like bureaucracy, death is always subject to delay (p. 9). It is in such moments of mordant humour that *Antes que anochezca* transcends the scepticism which its details may provoke and inspires the respect due the memoirs of a dignified survivor.

4. CONDITIONS OF REPRESENTABILITY

In chapter 6 of *The Interpretation of Dreams*, Freud gives two examples of 'reversal into opposite' characteristic of the dreamwork.[20] The first is the 'Up and Down Dream' (p. 288). A man notices that as he carries a woman up a staircase she becomes lighter, not heavier, the further they go; it is as if the positions of up above and down below have been reversed. In the second, 'Goethe's Attack on Herr M.', the dreamer believes that the celebrated author has denigrated his unknown friend, whereas in fact it is the other way round. As Freud puts it in Strachey's translation: '"just the reverse" has to be put straight', by drawing out the 'contemptuous indications of the phrase "turning one's back on something"' (the German *Kehrseite* meaning literally 'backside'). 'It is remarkable to observe', notes Freud dryly, 'how frequently reversal is employed in dreams arising from repressed homosexual impulses' (p. 327).

This last phrase is taken from the section of the chapter on 'the means of representation' under (psychic) censorship. I have argued that a similar rhetoric of reversal occurs in US and UK responses to homosexuality in Cuba. Turning their backs on victims of oppression, refusing to see what a recent critic has called 'the palpable dignity of abused survivors',[21] film scholars have claimed up is down and light dark. Ironically, it is also a technique consciously employed by Almendros and Arenas: in *Mauvaise conduite* Castro's inspection of a labour camp is compared to that of the grand lady visiting her serfs; in the first story of Arenas's novel *Viaje a la Habana* (written as the laws on extravagance and improper conduct came into force) a bizarre couple are terrified by the notion that someone in Cuba may not be watching them as they parade through the streets in impossibly extravagant costumes.[22] Repeating and reversing the trial of visibility to which so many were to be subjected, shadowing the trek over the island which Arenas himself undertook in his quest for the freedom to love and to write, the novel reveals that 'in the right hands' reversal is an incomparable technique for showing 'the way things are' in a dictatorship. There is thus a certain collusion between fiction and the real, with the oblique allegory of the novel pointing perhaps more clearly than the all too explicit autobiography to what is not seen, to what does not let itself be seen, to the space, at once necessary and impossible, that lies beyond the frame.[23]

The critique of representation derived from theorists such as the early Barthes and Althusser was originally devised to combat those ideological state apparatuses which served to exile dissident viewpoints outside a self-mythologizing bourgeois culture. As long as 'I see' meant 'I understand', received aesthetic and political criteria were mutually supporting and impossible to challenge. We have seen that Anglo-American critics retrained that powerful critique on the victims of totalitarianism whose access to any form of representation was meagre indeed: Almendros struggled to fund and distribute his documentaries, especially in the US; Arenas's literary production, undertaken under such tragically reduced circumstances, received only the slightest of financial rewards. Both were branded as agents of the CIA or worse. Ten years after the release of *Mauvaise conduite* it is clear that a certain idea of 'Cuba' served as a projection or (in Chanan's word) an 'identification' for leftists in the US and the UK who suffered in the 1980s under triumphalist governments of the Right. For France and Spain, on the other hand, which spent most of the decade under self-styled Socialist administrations, Cuba had ceased for many to be the fetish it had been in the 1960s, when the exiled Almendros had been subject to barracking from leftist intellectuals on his arrival in Barcelona.[24] Much better versed in Marxism than their North American counterparts, French intellectuals were also more active in articulating alternative forms of resistance associated with a certain postmodernism: from the Levinas-derived 'respect for the other' of Finkielkraut to the celebration of the 'little narratives' of the Gulag by Lyotard.

I have suggested, however, that such national differences are psychic as well as historical. Reversing testimony into its opposite, Anglo-American critics, troubled perhaps by homosexual impulses which had been 'repressed' in both senses of the word, refused that process of identification which Almendros offered them all too nakedly in *Mauvaise conduite*.[25] However, if homosexual relations and identities vary from one culture to another, that is no excuse for failing to respond to the truth of the face. What is required is a critical identification which is (as Freud suggests once more) no mere hysterical imitation of the symptom, but rather a quest for the historical causes of repression. For the challenge and the danger of the other's body is that in Arenas's words, 'being oneself it can give us the pleasure of being another' (*Viaje*, p. 148). On the beach, that most unproductive of locations, bathing in light, that most neglected of resources, we may come to share with Almendros and Arenas the pleasures and perils of visibility, the vulnerability of the artist who seeks, naively, obstinately, passionately to speak the truth.

NOTES

1 Néstor Almendros, *Man with a Camera* (London: Faber, 1984); French edition, 1980; Spanish, 1982.

2 Reinaldo Arenas, *Antes que anochezca* (Barcelona: Tusquets, 1992).

3 'Les Films du mois: Néstor Almendros et Orlando Jiménez Leal', *Cinématographe* 98 (March 1984), p. 26.

4 Reprinted as 'Almendros and Documentary' in *Sight and Sound* (Winter 1985–6), pp. 50–4.

5 Sean Cubitt, *City Limits* (11 January 1985), p. 23; see also Cubitt's interview with Almendros and Michael Chanan in the same issue, 'Cuba libre?', p. 14.

6   B. Ruby Rich, 'Bay of Pix', *American Film* 9, (July/August 1984), pp. 57–9.

7   See Almendros's and Jiménez Leal's response to Rich, 'Improper Conduct', *American Film*, vol. 9, no. 10 (September 1984), pp. 18, 70–1. Gutiérrez Alea's *Fresa y chocolate* ridicules the constant repetition of advances in standards of education and health invoked here by Rich.

8   Rich does not mention that *Improper Conduct* is directed not to the US, but to a French TV audience, as is revealed by its opening sequence (the defection of Cuban ballet dancers in Paris).

9   Michael Chanan, *The Cuban Image* (London: BFI, 1985).

10 For Cabrera Infante's account of ICAIC, *P.M.* and *Improper Conduct* see his 'Cuba's Shadow', in *Film Comment* (May/June 1985), pp. 43–5.

11 The review has recently been republished in the collection of writings which Almendros edited just before his death, *Cinemanía* (Barcelona: Seix Barral, 1992).

12 Reproduced in Almendros and Jiménez Leal's companion volume to the film, *Conducta impropia* (Madrid: Playor, 1984), p. 177.

13 *Monthly Film Bulletin* (July 1984), pp. 220–1.

14 One exception is the review by 'Hitch.' in US trade journal *Variety* (25 April 1984), which calls it 'an important film of lasting value' which 'clearly can find its place before sophisticated audiences in congenial art theaters.'

15 Michel Celeminski, review, *Cinématographe* 98 (March 1984), pp. 27–8. Alain Menil also gives a commentary on p. 28.

16 Charles Tesson, 'Docteur Fidel et Mister Raul', *Cahiers du Cinéma* 358 (April 1984), pp. 47–8.

17 See also the favourable review by 'M. C.' in *Positif* 279 (May 1984), p. 72–3.

18 Anonymous, 'Néstor Almendros gana el premio del Festival de Cine de Derechos Humanos de Estrasburgo', *Cineinforme* 130 (May 1984), p. 9.

19 Tomás Robaina, 'Carta acerca de *Antes que anochezca*, autobiografía de Reinaldo Arenas', *Journal of Hispanic Research* 1 (1992), pp. 152–6; this text was handed to Catherine Davies in Havana by the author and is introduced by Verity Smith. Robaina writes that one copy of Arenas's book has been circulated amongst members of the official Cuban writers' union (UNEAC) by José Rodríguez Feo.

20 Sigmund Freud, *The Interpretation of Dreams* (New York: Basic, 1960).

21 Ana M. López, 'Cuban Cinema in Exile: The "Other" Island', *Jump Cut* 38 (1993), p. 56. López is discussing Almendros's later documentary *Nadie escuchaba* (Nobody Listened, 1988) at this point. Her account of *Improper Conduct* is heavily dependent on Chanan and Rich.

22 Reinaldo Arenas, *Viaje a la Habana* (Miami: Universal, 1990); this first story ('Que trine Eva') is dated 1971. For this unrepentant exhibitionism compare his volume of poetry, *Voluntad de vivir manifestándose* (Madrid: Betania, 1989).

23 For Arenas's fusion of history and fiction see his historical reworkings *El mundo alucinante* (Mexico: Diógenes, 1978); and *La loma del ángel* (Barcelona: Dador, 1989). For Hispanic autobiography as 'mask' and 'impossibility' see Sylvia Molloy, *At Face Value: Autobiographical Writing in Spanish America* (Cambridge: Cambridge University Press, 1991), p. 1.

24 See Terenci Moix's memoir, 'Mi Néstor Almendros', *El País*, Madrid (7 March 1992), p. 11. Moix suggests that, in spite of his misfortunes, Almendros was less serious in private than he chose to reveal in his published writings.

25 As he notes in *Cinématographe* 98, March 1984, p. 26.

4

FRESA Y CHOCOLATE

(STRAWBERRY AND CHOCOLATE):

Cinema as Guided Tour

1. A CLASSICAL PHOTOLOGY

> Filled with malicious swipes against the Castro regime, [*Fresa y
> chocolate*] is a provocative but very humane comedy about sexual
> opposites and, with proper handling, could attract the *Wedding
> Banquet* crowd in cinemas worldwide.

So wrote *Variety* in its preview of the first Cuban film to focus on
homosexuality on the island.[1] The prediction proved correct: *Fresa
y chocolate* was to win prizes around the world and prove financially
successful. As 'the international breakthrough movie for Cuban
cinema' (*Variety* once more) it reveals that there exists abroad
a market for films, such as Ang Lee's or Gutiérrez Alea's, in which
gay-themed material is placed in a national context unfamiliar
to the foreign audience, whether that context is Taiwanese-
American or Cuban. I shall argue that this desire for homosexuality,
couched here in the form of cultural tourism, is also present in a
different, domestic form in the project of the film itself: the
attempt, persistent but impossible, to incorporate or assimilate
same-sex eroticism into the nationalist project of the Revolution,
from which it had once been so ostentatiously excluded.

If the international success of *Fresa y chocolate* is thus easy to
explain (with art-house audiences anxious to reconcile their
nostalgia for the Cuban political experiment with their sympathy
towards queer romance),[2] then the pervasive naturalism of the
film is more puzzling. Tomás Gutiérrez Alea, who shares directing

credit with Juan Carlos Tabío, is not only held to be an ethically serious director who is, nonetheless, wholly loyal to the regime's cultural policy;[3] he is also famous for films such as *Memorias de subdesarrollo* (Memories of Underdevelopment, 1968), which are characterized by radical experiment in cinematic form.[4] Is there a structural connection, then, between the unprecedented subject matter of this film and the unusual timidity of its mode of representation?

Fresa y chocolate takes the form of a chamber piece in which a flamboyant gay man (Diego: Jorge Perugorría) and a sober revolutionary (David: Vladimir Cruz) confront one another at length and repeatedly, debating their different conceptions of sexuality and nationality (Plate 10). It is clear from the outset that these conceptions are inextricable from conditions of representability and censorship; or in other words, that it is in the field of the visible, as much as in the wordy exchanges of the film's dialogue, that such struggles take place. Indeed, I shall argue that it is only in the perhaps unconscious recurrence of certain visual motifs (a towel, a flower) that a new reading of the film can emerge, one which transcends the rigid dichotomies and final sentimental synthesis of the overt narrative. If the aesthetic impoverishment of *Fresa y chocolate*, its overemphasis and demonstrativity, are transparent (with the dangerous desires of gay men and women requiring containment through an appeal to the unambiguous and privileged perspective of a heterosexual male), then still there is a certain visual surplus or remainder which suggests the identification of opposites that cannot be spoken aloud, an identification which is much clearer in the novella by Senel Paz on which the film is based.[5]

Gutiérrez Alea has claimed that the 'special addressee' of *Fresa y chocolate* is Néstor Almendros, whose *Mauvaise conduite* he had so bitterly attacked a decade earlier.[6] While this recantation could hardly be more untimely, coming as it does after the cinematographer's death, it raises the possibility of comparing the two films: Does *Fresa y chocolate* elude those theoretical naivetés of which its predecessor was accused? Does it undermine or reconfirm that 'straight line from the real to the visible' that critics such as Chanan so hotly contested?[7] Rather than simply dismissing the Marxist-derived project of a politics of representation, I hope to read *Fresa y chocolate* against and through the work of the French theorist to whom Chanan appealed in this context: Serge Daney.

Erratic and idiosyncratic, Daney offers no grand theory of the cinematic apparatus. But in his evolution from the militant engagement of the 1960s, through the psychoanalytic turn of the 1970s, to the ethics of embodiment of the 1980s, Daney stakes out an exemplary trajectory for film and television criticism. Moreover, as an openly gay writer, and, latterly, one living openly with AIDS, he addresses more attentively than most the relation between homosexuality and film. I shall argue, then, not only that Daney's diagnosis of the twilight of cinema (of its decline from vision to visuals) can account for the aesthetic timidity of *Fresa y chocolate*; but also that his version of a certain postmodern cinema as a 'guided tour' in which the director displays his cinematic props for the consumerist delight of the spectator points forward to a new reading of *Fresa y chocolate*, one which is not restricted by the limits of its technique.

The traditionalism and naturalism of *Fresa y chocolate* are all the more surprising when one looks at Gutiérrez Alea's own theoretical writings. In 'Dialectic of the Spectator'[8] (perhaps his most developed piece) we initially find a familiar militant paradigm: the revolutionary filmmaker must move from 'popular cinema' to a 'cinema of the people', from the purveyance of pure spectacle to the instigation of thought, and thus move the audience from contemplation to action (pp. 37, 46, 62). However, such changes in consciousness cannot be achieved by content alone: if Tarzan were to be replaced by a Socialist hero with whom the audience was absolutely to identify, the result would remain reactionary (p. 72). The cinematic experiment is a process of discovering or uncovering (*descubrir*), of rendering visible what was formerly obscured by the ideological anaesthesia of everyday life (p. 75). And while discontinuity editing or audiovisual counterpoint may serve to 'reveal new facts about reality', they soon become hackneyed (p. 77). Gutiérrez Alea thus proposes not the rejection but the incorporation of the fascinating blandishments of Hollywood, citing the Cuban motif of the *contracandela*: the small fire that is set on purpose in order to contain the advance of a conflagration in a cane field (p. 73). Fighting fire with fire and containing the dangerous 'surrender' (*entrega*) of the spectator to narrative cinema, the committed director assimilates or incorporates bourgeois techniques, using them to confront spectators with an image of themselves immersed in the world and thus provoke in them a crisis of consciousness (p. 83).

If Gutiérrez Alea is thus more willing than one might have supposed to appeal to such reactionary resources of film as identification, the problematic of visibility (of the supposed gap between knowledge and recognition, between perception and insight which remains to be bridged by Socialism) remains firmly in place. Yet if we look at the early essay by Daney to which Chanan referred, we find a very different account of the debate. 'Travail, lecture, jouissance'[9] begins with an extreme proposition of the 'crisis in the ideology of visibility' (p. 39). Cinema, writes Daney, is not a relation to the real or to the visible; the latter is always something else or other. The blind faith in the visible, the hegemony of the eye, is branded 'photology': the neutralization of duration and force through the illusion of simultaneity and filmic form. The confusion of vision and knowledge is thus deadly; it can culminate only in a cinema of transparent proposition (*évidence*) and resplendent truth typified by advertising (p. 40). More generally there are two modes of visibility in film: in the first, diversity is offered up as spectacle and thus slyly neutralized by the presentation of disparate elements ('men and monsters') in the same frame; in the second, more specifically cinematic, the materiality of film is reinscribed and the object, no longer self-evident, is neglected. While the first mode corresponds to classical cinema and the second to the modern film inaugurated by Rossellini, there is a third mode in which (as in Godard's *Le Mépris*), earlier innovations are simply simulated, in a postmodern overemphasis (p. 42).

It thus follows, then, that the critique of the innocence of vision which Chanan finds in this essay is but a starting point for Daney, who goes on to proclaim the exhaustion of that materialist attempt to renovate cinematic practice and to impose a labour (*travail*) of looking, which we might associate with Gutiérrez Alea and his Cuban colleagues. For Daney the future of figuration lies neither with a return to the innocent object of classical cinema, nor with a continued focus on the ideologically saturated object of materialist experiment, but rather with a third mode which he does not yet define. Moreover, the essay begins with a quote not from Marx but from Nietzsche, which claims that 'appearance' is no dead mask, but rather lived reality itself, embracing all that there is in its ironic and vital performance (p. 39). We could hardly be further from Gutiérrez Alea's earnest endeavour to uncover 'deeper levels of reality', nor from his pragmatic assimilation of past practice.

Plate 1   Ana Belén (Adela) in Mario Camus's *The House of Bernarda Alba*, 1987.

Plate 2   Victoria Peña (Martirio) in Mario Camus's *The House of Bernarda Alba*, 1987.

Plate 3   Irene Gutiérrez Caba (Bernarda) in Mario Camus's *The House of Bernarda Alba*, 1987.

Plate 4   Julieta Serrano (Mother Superior) and Cristina Sánchez Pascual (Yolanda) in Almodóvar's *Dark Habits*, 1983.

Plate 5 Chus Lampreave (Sister Rat) and Cristina Sánchez Pascual (Yolanda) in Almodóvar's *Dark Habits*, 1983.

Plate 6 Verónica Forqué (Kika) in Almodóvar's *Kika*, 1993.

Plate 7   Victoria Abril (Andrea) in Almodóvar's *Kika*, 1993.

Plate 8   Néstor Almendros and Orlando Jiménez Leal shooting *Improper Conduct*, 1984.

Plate 9   Armando Valladares in *Improper Conduct*, 1984.

Plate 10 Vladimir Cruz (David) and Jorge Perugorría (Diego) in Gutiérrez Alea's
Strawberry and Chocolate, 1993.

Plate 11 Vladimir Cruz (David) and Mirta Ibarra (Nancy) in Gutiérrez Alea's *Strawberry
and Chocolate*, 1993.

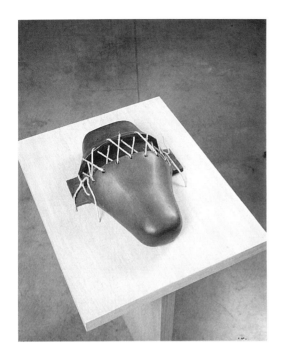

Plate 12   Pepe Espaliú's 'Untitled', 1989.

Plate 13   Pepe Espaliú's 'For Those Who No Longer Live in Me', 1992.

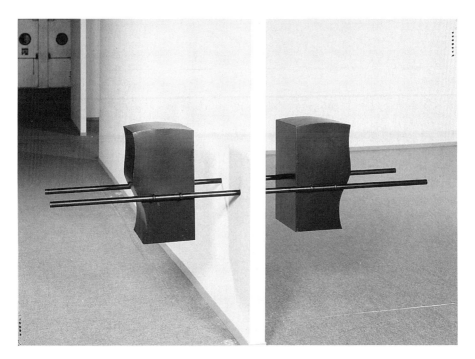

Plate 14   Pepe Espaliú's 'Carrying I', 1992.

Plate 15   Pepe Espaliú's 'Carrying', performance 1992.

Plate 16   Pepe Espaliú's 'The Nest', performance 1993 (*continues overleaf*).

Plate 16 (*continued*)   Pepe Espaliú's 'The Nest'.

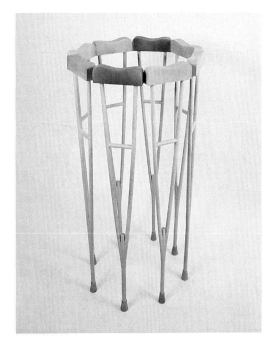

Plate 17 Pepe Espaliú's 'The Nest', 1993.

Plate 18 Pepe Espaliú's 'Rumi', 1993.

Plate 19   Emma Suárez (Lisa) in Julio Medem's *The Red Squirrel*, 1993.

Plate 20   Nancho Novo (Jota) and Carmelo Gómez (Félix) in Julio Medem's *The Red Squirrel*, 1993.

The opening sequences of *Fresa y chocolate* suggest a 'vision of the world' and 'practice of the look' (terms ridiculed by Daney), reminiscent of the most coercive regime of classical cinema. The pre-credit sequence has David and his fiancée Vivian arrive in the seedy hotel room where he plans to lose his virginity. After a first casually framed two shot, the spectator is firmly sutured into identification with David: he peers through a peephole at an energetic straight couple having sex in the adjoining bedroom (Vivian is in the bathroom) and later the camera pans slowly in a subjective shot across her naked back as she reclines in bed. This primacy of the heterosexual look or vision is repeated in the next sequence, which follows David's rejection by Vivian: when flamboyant queen Diego plants himself down at David's table in the Coppelia ice cream parlour, Diego is shown at first in medium shot (small in the frame), crosscut with an extreme close-up of David's dark, dismissive gaze. As the identification character David thus divides up the field of the visible for our consumption, whether it is pleasurable (the naked female) or unpleasurable (the clothed but flagrantly visible male homosexual). It is not simply, then, that within the terms of the film itself Cuba is represented as a place of constant and invasive surveillance (to be observed in public with a *loca* is in itself a perilous predicament); it is that the trial of visibility is retraced and thus reconfirmed by a classical photology: an equation of sight and knowledge predicated on the revelation of that which has hitherto been hidden (the coy fiancée's naked back; the revolutionary society's shameful deviants). Placing the Communist 'new man' and the effeminate bourgeois 'monster' in the same frame, Gutiérrez Alea offers a superficial diversity which is in fact neutralized by the falsely transparent *mise-en-scène* of naturalistic, narrative cinema.

This overemphasis or retracing of the already known in the form of a self-evident proposition (*évidence*) continues after Diego has tempted David back to his flat in elegantly decayed old Havana. Just as the two men are about to enter the building, a troupe of Young Communist Pioneers march past the doorway; and the couple are forced to hide in the stairwell in order to avoid (or so Diego claims) Nancy (Mirta Ibarra), the Vigilancia or Neighbourhood Watch representative (Plate 11). Once inside the cluttered apartment ('Welcome to my lair!'), David insists the door is left open. Diego unveils his friend Germán's heterodox sculptures (near life-size figures of saints) and a slow pan over the walls covered by cluttered and overlapping images (from framed photographs to abstract paintings) reproduces David's perspective on the location. As Diego brews the Indian tea, conspicuously contrasted in the dialogue with indigenous Cuban coffee, David lifts sheets to reveal more statues and removes from an envelope photographs which prove to be of a naked youth.

What is telling in this sequence is the acting out of a process of depth which Daney sees as typical of classical, illusionistic cinema: objects such as doors or windows serve as 'pivots', repeatedly raising and frustrating that desire to 'see more' beyond or behind the filmic image.[10] If, as Daney claims, cinema remains haunted by the memory of the studio in which it originated, then Diego's 'lair' is precisely that restricted and pseudo-theatrical space of classical *mise-en-scène* to which the action constantly returns. And if homosexuality is defiantly visible, superficial, in a typical displacement it is David who will come to reveal that 'more to see' demanded by the classical spectator of his objects: he later shows Diego (shows us) the first essays at fiction that he has hidden from others, the symptom of a true sensitivity hidden behind a falsely forbidding exterior.

Daney contrasts this simulated depth (of *mise-en-scène*, of characterization) not only with the 'flatness of the image' characteristic of modern, experimental cinema, but also with what he calls the sliding (*glissement*) of one image-object over the other, which he claims to find in a postmodern cinema dedicated not to demystifying the cinematic apparatus, but rather to exploring its genealogy (p. 175). Citing Syberberg and Ruiz as directors whose films are 'saturated' with culture and for whom the scenic backdrop is already itself an image, Daney tentatively proposes the 'baroque' as the third mode of filmic representation in which the successive stages of theatre, cinema and studio give way to the 'guided tour'.

It seems possible, then, that in the very transparency of its simulation of depth (in the reiterated movement with which it poses and removes cultural totems or obstacles), *Fresa y chocolate* might be read as an ironic staging of cultural capital. Thus Diego's accumulation of bourgeois commodities (fine tea and porcelain) is matched by his ostentatious exhibition, both visual and oral, of literary icons: placing himself in the queer lineage of Wilde, Gide and Lorca, seeing himself reflected in the photograph of 'the father of all Cubans' gay, baroque novelist Lezama Lima. When the backdrop is itself an image (Diego's walls are wholly covered by found materials) even the most fixed of cinematic objects will, as we shall see, begin to slip and slide one over the other. But that process is contained by a practice of opposition or contradiction which is parodically overdetermined. Thus the two principal characters are made to embody multiple differences: not just straight and gay, but also provincial and metropolitan, domestic and cosmopolitan, atheist and religious. As Daney claims of Visconti's *Ludwig* (another, grander guided tour of a cluttered cinematic property), *Fresa y chocolate* does not simply show (*montre*), it demonstrates (*démontre*), heavily gesticulating with its directorial hand.[11] Gutiérrez Alea shares a weakness for just such demonstration, which abolishes all suspense and surprise. The predictability of *Fresa y chocolate*'s plot (in which conflict cedes, inevitably, to reconciliation) is thus not simply a function of the schematic oppositions on which the narrative is based; it is also the result of Gutiérrez Alea's nostalgia for the studio, for the illusion of depth and the 'more to see' characteristic of classic cinema and impossible to revive today.

Why did the modernists, such as Rossellini, abandon illusionism after the destruction of Europe in the 1940s? In a gloss on Daney, Deleuze cites the supposed complicity between war and cinema, Hitler and Hollywood, exposed by Virilio.[12] Daney himself puts it less glibly: behind the seductive spectacle and public displays of the Nazis and Soviets lay another scene which would not be described and which would come to haunt later imaginations: the death camps (p. 174). The modern cinema's assumption of 'non-depth' as a weapon against the narrative illusionism and industrial alienation of commercial cinema was thus a political and ethical refusal of the 'hidden reverse' of the propagandistic *mise-en-scène* and the mass *tableaux vivants* of the theatre of war (p. 172). Rather than asking 'What is there to be seen behind?', experimental filmmakers posed the question: 'Can I withstand with my look what I am seeing?' Deprived of simulated depth (of exits or alibis) the screen becomes a pure surface or mirror in which the spectator seizes his or her look, as that of an intruder, as excess or surplus of the image.

Transposed into a slightly different language, this is not so far from the strategy proposed by Gutiérrez Alea in his early theoretical writings: the demystifying and revelatory *desgarramiento* or rupture by which spectators are confronted with themselves and their consciousness is put into crisis. The necessity of *Fresa y chocolate*'s naturalism thus becomes clear: by narrativizing explicitly, if discreetly, the oppression of homosexuals in Cuba, the film stages a domesticated *mise-en-scène* in which the unspeakable horrors of the other scene (out of shot, behind the door) are allowed to emerge into visibility, but only on condition that they do not trouble the heterosexual spectator. Rather the film provides a picturesque alibi for his look, which is not returned to him as if in a mirror. It follows that while Diego is allowed to invoke the UMAP camps, David can simply dismiss them as an 'error' of the Revolution.[13] The incorporation of homosexuality into a pre-existing concept of nationality is thus stage-managed in such a way as to avoid the contemplation or modification of either that nationality or the heterosexual masculinity from which it is inseparable. An emblematic scene here is when David stops to contemplate a shop window in which mannequins are dressed as bride and groom: his face, distorted, is reflected in the window. While such a sequence might have been used to suggest the implication of the character (of the audience) in a compulsory and commodified heterosexual *mise-en-scène*, it serves rather to deflect that self-knowledge on to an emphatic underlining of the boundary between hetero and homo: David tells us, in authoritative voice-over, that his friendship with Diego has been occasioned by his rejection by ex-fiancée Vivian. Queer companionship is thus preceded and underwritten by straight sexual frustration.

2. FROM VISION TO VISUALS

Fresa y chocolate is part funded by Spanish TV company Telemadrid. And in its insistence on explicitly addressing weighty issues it coincides with Daney's critique of film drama funded (and aesthetically contaminated) by television. For example, a British film such as *Another Country* also stages a self-conscious debate on homosexuality and betrayal, on the possibility of integrating excluded queers into the body politic.[14] The weightiness of the issue, however, is matched only by the film's indifference to properly filmic resources. For Daney, TV's fondness for the medium shot (*plan moyen*) suggests its inherent mediocrity; film, on the other hand, is always too close to or too far from its object, initiating an 'adventure of perception' (p. 212). While TV is 'about' the world, film is (or should be) 'with' it (p. 213). The mediocrity of *Fresa y chocolate*'s technique (its preference for medium shots, reverse angles and continuity editing) is thus consistent with its ideological project in which the (unexamined) pro-filmic object of homosexuality must be bound within the frame and cannot be allowed to transform existing modes of perception or simply accompany the camera on a journey whose aim is not mapped out in advance.

If the divide between homo and hetero must be rigorously policed even as an impeccably patriotic, 'democratically Communist' queer is admitted into the body politic, then the divide between masculine and feminine is yet more problematic. For as the film develops, the female characters prove to share a slippery, supplementary status: at once additions to and substitutes for the 'red queen' Diego. For example, as we have seen, Diego replaces Vivian as the sexless object of David's affections; but later she substitutes for him, as a ghostly echo or simulacrum: David and Vivian meet in a café, in an echo of David's encounter with Diego in the ice cream parlour; and Vivian is, like Diego, to abandon Cuba, although she is motivated more by consumerism than persecution. More important is Nancy. In her case the logic of the editing repeatedly implies at once an equation of femininity and male homosexuality and a compulsive substitution of the latter by the former. Thus the brief shot of the naked youth in the photograph is immediately interrupted by Nancy's entrance and first meeting with David; or again, a slow pan over David's naked torso from Diego's point of view cuts to a full-body shot of Nancy naked in the shower. Most transparently, the supper party at which Diego recreates for David's pleasure and profit the baroque dinner given in Lezama Lima's *Paradiso* (thus marking the high point of the latter's induction into a sensual and intellectual queer culture) is also attended by Nancy and is immediately followed by her seduction of David. Gay men and straight women are thus equated in their emotionalism (Nancy is sentimental, suicidal, superstitious), but they are not allowed to occupy the same place, must always substitute for one another in their attempts to procure the affection, indeed the attention, of the straight man for whose sentimental education they can only be vehicles: Nancy claims that she 'wants David to know love through her'. What cannot be allowed then and what would ultimately unite gay men and women is the possibility of a first-person feminine-identified narrative, in which Diego and Nancy might assume the position of photological mastery so effortlessly and unthinkingly granted David by *Fresa y chocolate*'s narrative structure, cinematography and editing.

I return to the supper party in a moment, contrasting Gutiérrez Alea's treatment of the scene with that of Senel Paz in the novella on which the film is based. But if the clichéd scenes of heterosexual romance such as David and Nancy spooning on the Malecón are prime examples of what Daney has called the 'filmed cinema'[15] of the guided tour ('a series of images which must be seen, recognized and . . . ticked off by the spectator-consumer'), there remains a spectral and more troubling couple whom I have not yet discussed: David and his handsome, homophobic roommate Miguel (Francisco Gattorno). Like Nancy, Miguel is transparently a vehicle of displacement for the film's homosexual panic and censorship mechanisms. Thus David's first visit to Diego's flat ends after David flees when Diego is about to tell him 'how [he] became queer' (an erotic narrative which is told in the novella but not in the film). Gutiérrez Alea cuts straight to David's denunciation of the 'dangerous' queer to the politically orthodox Miguel. But, curiously, there is a visual hook in this sequence implying an identification with the one it follows: Miguel (like David in Diego's flat) is bare-chested, with a towel around his neck. And if here Miguel substitutes for David as the addressee of a queer narration, in a later sequence he takes Diego's place in a burlesque of erotic admiration. After David has returned drunk on Diego's foreign whisky, Miguel (clad like David only in his underpants) holds him from behind under the shower, slapping him on the arse and coarsely complimenting him. The overt message here is the grossness of homophobic intolerance, so different to the cultured gentility of the homosexual who is its victim. But the seductive backlighting of this sequence evokes the heterosexual love scene between David and Vivian which begins the film; and Miguel's grappling with David, almost naked and from behind, is the repressed mirror image of the chaste, clothed hug between David and Diego with which the film will close. Hence, although Miguel identifies homosexuality with treachery ('How can you trust a man who is disloyal to his own sex?'), it is rather homophobia that opens up a space for betrayal and denial, by repeatedly asserting and denying the existence and the fascination of same-sex desire.

Miguel claims later that 'The Revolution doesn't take it up the arse.' It is clear, then, that homophobia does not simply sublimate homosexuality in order to police the libidinal *mise-en-scène*, but rather is wholly dependent on that same homosexuality in order to preserve its privilege. Ironically, then, it is only in Miguel's overt repression of homosexuality (as opposed to the sexless Diego's sublimation and containment of it) that specific sexual practices can be voiced. And the phantom of anality, invoked to hold men such as David in line, raises the possibility at least of a queer rereading (a re-eroticization) of a film as persistently and wilfully sexless as *Fresa y chocolate*. And here we may turn to Senel Paz's novella for corroboration. At first Paz seems simply to prefigure in literary terms the visual regime of Gutiérrez Alea: the first-person narration spoken by David ensures that masculine behaviour and its other are held rigorously separate as subject and object, respectively. And although the novella lacks major female characters (no Nancy or Vivian), there is still an equation of gay man and straight woman in the way in which Diego and a frustrated female admirer are said to regard David: their libidinous looks are compared to those of a cow licking the man's face (p. 11). But there is also an equation implied between Diego and a character absent from the film: Ismael, a second Communist official, to whom David betrays Diego. Ismael is conspicuously endowed with the same attribute lent Diego: a 'penetrating look'; and David predicts that theirs will be a friendship 'like that of brothers', that he may even repeat the Lezamian dinner party for his new friend (p. 32). Projected, then, into the impossible, potential space after the end of his narration (the space from which David looks back in omniscience on his relation with Diego), the future friendship with the enigmatic Ismael suggests, discreetly and ironically, a possibility unspeakable in *Fresa y chocolate*: a homosexuality which is not flagrantly visible and readily identified, a gay relation between masculine-identified men who are nonetheless fully and invisibly integrated into the revolutionary establishment.

I have argued that Paz's literary naturalism anticipates the classical cinematic conventions with which Gutiérrez Alea traps and thus neutralizes his big issue, holding man and monster within the same frame. But there is one point at which Paz's illusionism becomes forced, one thread which might unravel the seamless textual fabric. It is in the supper party scene where Paz reproduces verbatim and without quotation marks phrases from Lezama's *Paradiso*, whose banquet Diego is seeking to recreate:

significant here are three drops of beetroot juice, blood-red stains on the white table cloth.[16] While the set of *Fresa y chocolate* is crammed with details whose significance must be exhaustively explained to us, demonstrated unambiguously as part of the guided tour to the house of homosexuality, this tiny motif has no meaning except as an unacknowledged citation from Lezama, a sign to the wise reader of a cultural continuity recognizable only to initiates: it is shown only to those who have already learned to see. We are far here from Gutiérrez Alea's self-conscious pleas for tolerance and identification, far from the heavy-handed gesture in which his camera lingers on Lezama's framed photograph on the wall of Diego's lair into which we, as privileged spectators, have been invited. For Paz's defiant and discreet assertion of an uncontrollable intertextuality (of a citation unrestricted by quotation marks) raises the possibility of a promiscuous flow of text and of bodies, one unbounded by the conventions of classical realism or 'democratic communism'.

Returning to *Fresa y chocolate*, how then can we reread its more rigid and less pleasurable postures? Perhaps the answer is to follow the logic of the *contracandela* and fight fire with fire. I will suggest, then, finally, that *Fresa y chocolate*'s professions of Marxist orthodoxy can be counterpointed with an early piece by Daney written at the high point of his engagement with a militant politics of representation. In 'The Name of the Author', Daney and collaborator Jean-Pierre Oudart stage a relentless attack on another bourgeois narrative of homosexual sublimation: Visconti's *Death in Venice*.[17] They place the film in a tradition of 'critical realism' in which an overt critique of bourgeois decadence is deflected on to and masked by a problematics of individualism that ensures the repression of historical struggle (p. 307). In such auteurist works, history is seen only through the eyes of a privileged witness-narrator, who bears the look of the director himself, the former serving as the narcissistic object of the latter (p. 309). As in the classical cinema of Hollywood, this practice of exchange is foreclosed, as is genital sexuality, and the repressed political discourse is reinscribed in humanist and metaphysical terms, framed as the critical look of the director at 'his' world (p. 310). The limits of the *mise-en-scène* of 'critical realism' are thus precisely scenic, staked out by the conventions of bourgeois theatre; and the mythic cause of that *mise-en-scène*'s decadence is sexuality: as symptom, secret and truth (p. 312). The problem is that in this 'convergence of economic, erotic, and political' functions, this 'metaphorical merging of . . . economic positions and erotic roles' (p. 313), 'no specific political discourse is possible', as politics is exhausted by the drawing into visibility of sexuality as truth (as symptom, as secret) of the bourgeois subject.

Daney's and Oudart's model would appear wholly suited to the classical realism of *Fresa y chocolate* (as it is not to Gutiérrez Alea's earlier, experimentally modern cinema). Thus *Fresa y chocolate* uses a privileged witness figure, re-marked for art-house audiences as the specular object of the auteur (David–Gutiérrez Alea) to render a critique of the environment both inhabit. That critique, however, which is authorized by the name of the most prestigious director associated with Castro's regime, fails to address the structural reasons for revolutionary homophobia, reinscribing a properly political question in terms of the conflict between individuals (David and Diego; David and Miguel) and sublimating that conflict into metaphysical terms: an abstract and wholly disembodied request for universal tolerance. Moreover, by replaying the clichéd equation of homosexuality and bourgeois decadence in the person of the fastidious, tea-sipping Diego, *Fresa y chocolate* precludes any specific political discourse by masking it in the gaudy show of sexual dissidence: Diego's flamboyance hides the fact that, even within the terms of the film's overt narrative, it is not homosexuality but the slightest sign of resistance to officialdom that is intolerable to the regime: Diego is compelled to leave Cuba not on account of his sexual offences, but because of the letter he writes to the authorities defending his friend Germán's right to exhibit the art works he has made. But if sexuality is all too visible, an alibi for a pervasive political repression which cannot be acknowledged, it is also sublimated, with genital activity posed as the limit of critical realism, as foreclosed as is the practice of exchange whereby the spectator 'buys into' the filmic economy only under the patronage of a prestigious auteur and his narcissistic (heterosexual) object-witness.

In *Death in Venice* a bourgeois anti-hero sacrifices himself to a sexless and unrequited love for a youthful aristocrat: the disavowal of genitality masks both the identification between auteur and witness-subject and the erotic relation between auteur and libidinal addressee-object. For Daney and Oudart this foreclosure of sexuality (of the dirt and contamination of sexual organs) is displaced on to the decor: a crumbling, plague-ridden Venice

(p. 318). The failure of this denial, however, is shown in its obsessive overemphasis:

> Visconti has been concerned not to deny homosexuality, but to make sure that one of its characteristics (the scatological) never affects the film's erotic scene, but is constantly displaced on to all the other scenes. These surplus elements of the film, its (scato-logical) excrescences etc. – and this is their function – only encroach into all the scenes of the film the better to protect *one* scene, which is occupied by a character (Tadzio [the youthful object]) as clean and translucent as everything around him is corroded by putrefaction. (p. 322)

There is thus a double repression typical of Freud's aetiology of paranoia in this direct passage from repression to sublimation. The proposition: 'I (a bourgeois) love him (a proletarian) – because he is dirty' is doubly denied thus: 'He is not a proletarian, he is precisely the opposite, an aristocrat'; and 'It is not he who is dirty, it is I'. For Daney and Oudart, then, the barred question of *Death in Venice* is not homosexuality per se, but its scatological and genital component, fantasized and repressed as the dirty and shameful (but fascinating because lost) part of the social body, the proletarian (p. 323).

In *Fresa y chocolate* a decadent bourgeois also contracts a sexless and sublimated love for a young, pure proletarian: the very first scene of the film serves only to establish David's innocence of sexuality. But (unlike *Death in Venice*) it is the love object who is also the privileged witness to the decadence of his milieu; and his innocence and virtue serve only to veil the identification between the seasoned and sophisticated auteur and his callow alter ego. Moreover, the insistent and implausible chastity of the central scene is, as in Visconti, structurally determined by the foreclosure of homosexual genitality, whose supposed dirtiness is neurotically projected on to all of the other scenes: Vivian and Nancy are rendered impure by their sexual experience; Miguel is tainted by his recourse to scatological language. Most specifically, when Diego, in his habitual role of arbiter of elegance, tells David that the architectural beauty of Old Havana is 'sinking into shit' we cut to a montage sequence in which David is shown against a number of handsome, crumbling and finally decrepit buildings. It is not simply, then, that the sexual masks the political (with homophile aestheticism standing in for a critique of the Revolution's economic failure); it is rather that genital or scatological homosexuality is unconsciously equated with the excrescence and contamination of that social world which condemns it to repression or sublimation. It is not homosexuality per se that is barred, but rather any suggestion that its incorporation into the political body (as that body's lost, dirty and shameful part) might transform that body in political rather than merely cultural or aesthetic terms.

The double repression of Gutiérrez Alea is thus quite different to that of Visconti. For *Fresa y chocolate*, as I have argued, cannot tolerate the first person and thus begins from the second stage of paranoid displacement: 'I (a man) love him (a man)' has become 'He (a man) loves me'. And the film's fatal fascination with bourgeois decadence (its heavy-handed weakness for the guided tour of cosmopolitan cultural capital) betrays a further denial: it is not that Diego loves David because he (Diego) is decadent, but rather quite the reverse: the proletarian comes to love opera and supper parties, tea and literature. Neglecting the troublesome dirt and putrefaction of the disturbingly material social world outside (in which, David tells us in voice-over, 'people think of nothing but sex'), Gutiérrez Alea delights with his alter ego–witness in the elite pleasures of high culture. Just as in a bourgeois and repressed Europe the distance from middle to working class facilitated the eroticization of the divide which at once separated and united them, so in proletarian and puritan Cuba the abjection (expulsion, denigration) of the bourgeoisie renders their remainder curiously seductive: as David listens to Maria Callas, slumped in the armchair Diego reserves for Donne and Cavafy, his eyes rise to the heavens in a kind of mystic abandon. It is a delivery (*entrega*) of the self, given up to the rapture of communion with great (European) art.

In his experimental films Gutiérrez Alea exploited audiovisual counterpoint (a certain discontinuity between image and sound tracks). Typical of the overemphasis of *Fresa y chocolate* (its compulsion to demonstrate) is the use of music simply to reinforce particular shots or plot points, which are then in the redoubling characteristic of cultural tourism alluded to explicitly in the dialogue: thus we not only listen to Ignacio Cervantes's 'Farewell to Cuba' and 'Lost Illusions' as Diego secretly plans to leave the island, but also hear Diego identify the pieces for David (for us) and remark on the composer's expulsion from the island by the Spanish. But if this is the auditory equivalent of the visual process by which Gutiérrez Alea serves up aesthetically pleasing images to be, in Daney's words, 'recognised' and 'ticked off' by the spectator-consumer, there remain excesses or excrescences, motifs in the film which circulate freely and without self-conscious underlining, often against the logic of the narrative itself. One of these was, I suggested, the towel which is displaced from the shoulders of love-object and cultural pupil David to critic and homophobe Miguel, thus lending a dangerous and unacknowledged eroticism to the latter. Another is the sunflower. When Diego first sits down at David's table in the ice cream parlour he is holding a bunch of sunflowers; when they first arrive at his flat he hands them to David to hold while he pays the taxi driver. Later, Nancy awakes David in Diego's flat, where he has passed a drunken but chaste night, with a sunflower in her hand; and David himself arrives at the flat for a final visit with sunflowers, only to discover Miguel interrogating Diego. Passing from hand to hand, room to room, man to woman, and straight to gay, the sunflower (unsymbolized and unrecognized) seems to suggest that promiscuous flow of text and bodies I identified in Paz's insistent but unacknowledged citations from Lezama. It embodies a prelude to erotic action, an action that is undifferentiated and always deferred. As such it cannot figure as an item on the guided tour to the cultural monuments prized as the products of sublimated sexuality.

In one of his last texts Daney presented himself as a *passeur*: at once a ferry man and a guide, leading visitors across dangerous zones and forbidden frontiers.[18] This sense of the journey is not simply a meditation on his own status as a passionate lover of cinema and his 'destiny as a homosexual' (as a man who 'has no more than his own body . . . a body that he does not take care of, that he treats as a friendly machine'). It is also a reference to his understanding of cinema as an adventure of or in perception that accompanies the event it images, and which (unlike television) is not 'about', but 'with'. Open to pleasure and yet devoid of that self-conscious hedonism which Daney saw as a 'war machine' or 'ideological show', the model of filmmaker and critic as *passeur* provides both a path for future queer cinemas and an antidote to the stultifying claustrophobia of Diego's lair and Gutiérrez Alea's demonstrative cinema of ideas. If we must abandon, then, as Gutiérrez Alea has, the modern, materialist experiment of anti-illusionism, we cannot simply return to classic realism without always remembering, and most particularly in the case of Cuba, that behind the screen (the door, the window) lie the death camps: that off-screen space which can never be shown, but the effects of whose repression are everywhere. The challenge then (for cinema, for Cuba) is to operate a genealogy of the image which does not simply demystify it as the old Marxian dogmas of *Cahiers* and Gutiérrez Alea would suggest; rather it would initiate a productive and historical slippage, free of the aestheticism and academicism of the guided tour and based not on the visuals of cultural tourism, served up for the art houses worldwide, but on the vision of a newly democratized civil society.

NOTES

1 *Variety* (21 February 1994), p. 48.

2 In one of the very few critical press accounts of the film, Antonio Elorza points out the hypocrisies of 'nostalgic leftists' who claim (as the Franco regime had of Spain) that 'Cuba is different' and does not deserve the democratic rights which other nations take for granted: 'Sabores de un helado', *El País* (26 May 1994).

3 Gutiérrez Alea and Senel Paz (author of the short story on which *Fresa y chocolate* is based) were amongst the signatories of an open letter to Castro on the thirtieth anniversary of the Revolution which was published in *Granma* on 30 December 1988. The letter, praising the 'freedom' which is the 'source of artistic creation' in Cuba and pledging eternal allegiance to Fidel ('today and always'), was the unacknowledged response to the letter campaigning for a plebiscite on Castro's continuing rule, which was signed by Cuban exiles and foreign artists and intellectuals; see Reinaldo Arenas and Jorge Camacho, *Un plebiscito a Fidel Castro* (Madrid: Betania, 1990). The *Granma* letter is reproduced on p. 78.

4 The script of *Memorias* is published as *Memories of Underdevelopment* (New Brunswick and London: Rutgers University Press, no date given); introduction by Michael Chanan.

5 Senel Paz, *El lobo, el bosque, y el hombre nuevo* (Mexico: Era, 1991). This edition carries an endorsement from prestigious Mexican intellectual Carlos Monsiváis.

6 José Antonio Evora, 'Díos nos perdone; digo, Diego, en su nombre', in *Tomás Gutiérrez Alea: poesía y revolución* (Filmoteca Canaria, 1994), p. 211.

7 Michael Chanan, *The Cuban Image* (London: BFI, 1985), p. 103. For discussion see chapter 3, above.

8 Gutiérrez Alea, 'Dialéctica del espectador', in *Poesía y revolución*, pp. 33–133.

9 Serge Daney and Jean-Pierre Oudart, 'Travail, lecture, jouissance', *Cahiers du Cinéma* 222 (July 1970), pp. 39–51. (Daney's contribution, 'Sur Salador', pp. 39–43.)

10 Serge Daney, 'La Rampe (bis)', in *La Rampe: cahier critique 1970–82* (Paris: Cahiers du Cinéma/Gallimard, 1983), p. 171. Daney's history of film here owes much to Deleuze.

11 Serge Daney, review of *Ludwig* in *Ciné journal* (Paris: Cahiers du Cinéma, 1986), p. 168.

12 Gilles Deleuze, 'Optimisme, pessimisme, et voyage: lettre à Serge Daney', in *Ciné journal*, pp. 5–6.

13 For a fictional account of the camps, and a defiant vindication of homoerotic fantasy *in extremis*, see Reinaldo Arenas, *Arturo, la estrella más brillante* (Barcelona: Montesinos, 1984). For an account of the 'sanatoria' to which Cuba has confined people with HIV, see Nancy Scheper-Hughes and Robert Herrick, 'Ethical Tangles', *New Internationalist* (May 1992), p. 35.

14 Serge Daney 'La Télé anglaise fait du cinéma', in *Ciné journal*, p. 212. For a collection of Daney's pieces on television see *Le Salaire du zappeur* (Paris: Ramsay, 1988).

15 Serge Daney, 'Falling Out of Love', *Sight and Sound* 2.3 (1992), p. 16.

16 Emilio Bejel calls attention to this unacknowledged quotation (as he does to the identification of Ismael with Diego) in 'Senel Paz: homosexualidad, nacionalismo, y utopía', *Plural* 269 (February 1994), pp. 62, 65. Bejel's article is illustrated by inappropriate woodcuts of heterosexual coupling.

17 Serge Daney and Jean-Pierre Oudart, 'The Name of the Author (on the "Place" of Death in Venice)', in Nick Browne, ed., *Cahiers du Cinéma: Volume 3: 1969–72 The Politics of Representation* (London: Routledge/BFI, 1990), pp. 307–24.

18 Serge Daney, 'Film Buff on a Journey' (undated text reproduced in folder on the occasion of the second annual Serge Daney Lecture at the 23rd Rotterdam Film Festival; consulted on microfiche at BFI, London).

PART III

Spanish Revisions

5

FATAL STRATEGIES:

The Representation of AIDS in the Spanish State

1. BECOMING VISIBLE

Spain has the highest increase in rate of HIV transmission in Europe; and it has the second highest incidence of HIV infection of any European Union country.[1] Yet the epidemic has been over-whelmingly silent, invisible. In Spanish cinema (still substantially state-supported), there have been no mainstream films which have served to promote discussion of AIDS in the public sphere; nor have there been major independent filmmakers willing or able to tackle the theme. And if there are no obvious Spanish equivalents of, say, Cyril Collard in France or Derek Jarman in Britain, nor are there intellectuals or academics known for their commitment to analysing representations of the syndrome: no Cindy Patton, Douglas Crimp or Simon Watney. Even in the late 1980s and early 1990s, gay commentators could note the continuing unwillingness of the habitués of the burgeoning commercial gay ghettos of Madrid and Barcelona even to discuss the epidemic, let alone show solidarity towards those affected most severely by it.[2]

Yet the political and cultural climate of the Spanish state in the 1980s might have seemed propitious both to AIDS activism and artistic expression. While Britain and the US experienced, in Jeffrey Weeks's words, 'an irresolvable contradiction between the needs of people with AIDS and the political imperatives of New Right regimes',[3] Spain enjoyed a social democratic government

committed, in principle, to progressive policies in the varied fields
of sexual object choice and feminism, drug use and racism.
Moreover, the endemic weakness of the Spanish Right (at least
until the elections of 1993) and the relative absence of populist,
tabloid journalism suggested a certain consensus around public
health policy and inhibited the grossest homophobic outbursts
experienced in other countries.[4] It may be that (as Deborah
Lupton has argued in the somewhat similar case of Australia)
'loss of interest in the issue proved more damaging than did high
levels of controversy'.[5]

Yet, if the Spanish epidemic seems more stubbornly invisible
than most and if (as Sander Gilman has suggested) any epidemic
must be read for its 'particular, national qualities',[6] it is clear that
AIDS raises questions that problematize the visual field and forms
of representation in general: the invisible virus, whose relation
to visible marks on the body is irreducibly complex; the trial of
visibility to which PWAs are subjected, in which external condition
is read for signs of supposed internal essence; and the problem
of representing those who are affected without intrusion or
voyeurism, without collusion with a society in which the photographic image and printed text are valued means of discipline and
punishment. No one has described the double bind characteristic
of the 'look of AIDS' more effectively than Simon Watney:

> The 'look' of AIDS guarantees that it is made visible . . . as if it were
> a unitary phenomenon, stamping its 'victims' with unmistakable
> and irrefutable signs of the innately degenerate. We thus 'see'
> AIDS under two guises. First, as the 'AIDS virus', materialized by
> the technologies of computer graphics and electron microscopy,
> floating like some alien spacecraft in a dense space of violently
> saturated colour. Secondly we 'see' AIDS in living bodies which
> have been all but stripped of the sensual luxury of flesh . . . Such
> images embody the entire cultural agenda of AIDS at its most
> concentrated, efficient, and revealing.[7]

Caught between the micro (virology) and the macro (epidemiology),
AIDS resists visibility except in frames of reference that are
violently imposed on those who have first been made unbearably
vulnerable.

But if AIDS is, in the Spanish state, doubly invisible (for reasons
both national and international) then, given the almost complete
absence of studies in the field, the initial questions to be posed of

representations of the epidemic are at once simple and immediate: who, how and why. In this piece I will consider the work of gay male writers and artists, most of whom remain relatively little known even within Spain itself. Starting with the only book to my knowledge to have dealt in detail with the art and literature of AIDS in Spain (Juan Vicente Aliaga and José Miguel G. Cortés's *De amor y rabia* [Of Love and Rage]),[8] I go on to examine three figures considered to a greater or lesser degree in that book: poet and essayist Alberto Cardín; novelist and journalist Eduardo Haro Ibars; and finally (and at greatest length) conceptual artist and video filmmaker Pepe Espaliú. All three died of the effects of AIDS in the 1990s. What I would prefer to stress, however, is their enforced marginality. Just as *De amor y rabia* appeared with a provincial academic press and initially received little press coverage, so Cardín and Haro often published with small presses, and their work did not receive the support of an organized gay community of the US style. Likewise, the consolidation of Espaliú's reputation with a one-man show at the prestigious national museum of the Reina Sofía Art Centre occurred only posthumously, and even then was marred by controversy. Yet if my chosen figures were deprived of some of the support networks familiar to gay men in other countries, all three were effortlessly cosmopolitan, with Cardín and Espaliú fully conversant with the knottiest French theory and Haro intent on recreating William Burroughs's dystopias in Madrid, complete with alien spacecraft and violently saturated colour.

After who, the second question is how. The representations of AIDS produced by the figures I have chosen are quite different to those characteristic of the US or the UK. Where English-speakers respond to the urgency of the health crisis with direct and literal means (exemplified, perhaps, by the unadorned sans serif typeface favoured by Gran Fury), the Spanish tend to appeal to indirect and metaphorical techniques (exemplified, perhaps, by Espaliú's resonant and enigmatic performance of 'Carrying', to which I return later). Likewise, while the former are pragmatic and committed (with artists proclaiming, famously, that 'art is not enough'), the latter are more abstract and theoretical, seeking solace in Artaud or Lacan. Finally, while the former are positive and life-affirming, the latter stress the need to achieve a reconciliation with death, even to the extent of replicating those myths of AIDS which educators seek most energetically to undermine: the generalized horror of the body and of physicality; the fantasy of unlimited transmission (in Haro, by mosquito); the obsession with decay and putrefaction. I call this tendency (after Baudrillard) 'fatal strategies', in the twin sense, suggested by his translator, of inevitability and mortality.[9] In Baudrillard's words, the fatal strategy:

> combat[s] obscenity with its own weapons. To the more true than true we will oppose the more false than false. We will not oppose the beautiful and the ugly; we will seek what is more ugly than the ugly: the monstrous. We will not oppose the visible to the hidden; we will seek what is more hidden than the hidden: the secret.
> (p. 185)

Clearly, there are problems with Baudrillard's writings on AIDS itself, which seem offensively trivial and opportunistic. Yet the fatal strategy seems to correspond to the practice of Spanish artists and intellectuals, and not merely because some (such as Vicente Molina Foix) reveal a close familiarity with Baudrillard's work. Taking their pleasure in immoral ecstasy and spirals of intensity, insisting on the monstrous and the secret, Spanish writers and artists also propose a new ethics of sexual relations and of artistic representation, one that is made all the more urgent by its production in the shadow of mortality.

It is precisely this reading of AIDS as fatality (as fate and as death) that Anglo-American activists and scholars have struggled hardest to dislodge. Simon Watney has written: 'It is the image of fatality itself which people with AIDS have done most to challenge.'[10] The recurrence of the fatal strategy in Spanish responses to the epidemic, as in Haro's apocalyptic science fictions or Espaliú's coffinlike sculptures, is thus deeply disturbing. However, somewhat contradictory to this claim, the equally characteristic Spanish view, voiced by Espaliú himself,[11] is that while North Americans have responded to the epidemic above all with rage, the Spanish response has been one of love. I will suggest that this love is indeed compatible with the fatal strategy and manifests itself in the recurrent motifs of the remainder and the prosthesis: the former suggests a respect for the body and its products in their very abjection, even unto death; the latter suggests a supplement to the body, which permeates its once hermetic membranes, breaching the boundary between self and other.

Having established the identities of the figures to be studied and sketched the nature of their response (who and how), a more intransigent question remains: why. Why has AIDS in the Spanish state been so virulent and yet given rise to so few cultural expressions? Three possibilities arise. The first is the Spanish pattern of transmission. Cindy Patton has warned us, most particularly in the case of Africa, that we should be suspicious of supposed nationally specific epidemiological models which are in fact the result of the prejudices and projections of external observers.[12] It remains the case, however, that official figures (often tardy and unreliable)[13] claim that the proportion of transmissions deriving from IV drug use is much higher in Spain than in the US or Northern Europe, and that reported transmission by male-to-male sex is correspondingly lower.[14] With drug users even less likely than gay men in Spain to view themselves as a community with a right to public self-expression, the paucity of artistic representation of the syndrome might seem inevitable. Likewise, the relative lack of formal infrastructure or of a tradition of public speech in a putative Spanish gay community would problematize both the reach of health-care education and the production of literature, art or film around the epidemic. Finally, the fragmentation of the Spanish state, with the multiple autonomous regions competing for scarce resources[15] and the central authorities offering only fitful attempts at nationwide campaigns, tends perhaps to discourage collective awareness and collaboration even between very similar groups of committed artists from whom collective action might be expected: it seems characteristic that in spite of the relatively little work on AIDS produced in the visual arts, there is no overlap between the artists treated by Juan Vicente Aliaga in *De amor y rabia* and those who took part in an unrelated group exhibition on AIDS in Barcelona in 1993,[16] the same year that Aliaga's book was published in Valencia.

Inversely, however, the fragmentation of the Spanish state provides the opportunity for interventions at a local level of a kind favoured by many health educators: Ricardo Lorenzo and Héctor Anabitarte begin their book on AIDS in Spain with an account of a controversial distribution of condoms timed to coincide with Pamplona's famous local festivities, under the slogan: 'Sanfermín, Sancondón' (p. 5). If Spanish AIDS is thus a postmodern pandemic in its refusal to respond to such grand narratives as community action versus government inaction and in its decentredness and discontinuity, then it might also be postmodern in the opportunity it offers, still and much too late, for flexible and local forms of resistance.[17] These might be of interest to English-speaking activists such as Patton and Watney, who are themselves sceptical of 'the limits of community' and 'humanist pathos', respectively.[18] An initial hypothesis would be, then, that the weakness of identity politics in Spain has rendered the Spanish more vulnerable to HIV transmission by failing to create a sense of responsibility to and solidarity with others. However, the very complexity of such local conditions (in which even openly gay writers see no cause for celebrating Pride[19] and can take no pleasure in 'becoming visible')[20] have required complex responses from intellectuals and artists, responses which cannot be reduced to Anglo-American precedents. It is these fatal strategies that underscore the figures I examine: the remainder, which commemorates the difference between what was and what is left; and the prosthesis, which marks and erases the boundary between what is one's own and what is the other's.

2. OF LOVE AND RAGE: CARDÍN AND HARO IBARS

On the front cover of *De amor y rabia* is an untitled graphic work by Pepe Espaliú of 1993 in which a pencil trace spirals down towards an oval form reminiscent of a nest or a body cavity; on the back is a photo detail borrowed from Douglas Crimp and Adam Rolston's *AIDS Demo Graphics* in which a furious New Yorker punches the air wearing a T-shirt with the slogan: 'I do exist: Commissioner Joseph can't count'.[21] There could be no more evident example of that opposition between the oblique and the direct which I suggested was typical of the contrast between US and Spanish responses to the epidemic. However, the very presence of the US photo on the jacket reveals the familiarity of the book's editors with North American cultural politics, which is by no means alien to them; and English-speakers will find much in *De amor y rabia* to remind them of their own histories of AIDS.

The first similarity is a tale of government inaction and media indifference. In his account of press and TV representations of AIDS in Spain, Alberto Mira draws attention to the prolonged silence of public health authorities. The first state campaign did not begin until 1987, when TV spots featured animated humanoids demonstrating modes of transmission with the punning slogan 'Sí da, no da' (Yes it does; no it doesn't). So humorous and underplayed was this campaign, however, that its effect was negligible (p. 148).[22] And if once AIDS had been projected into the future ('It will never happen here'), now it remained in another country: it was not the death of Spanish poet Jaime Gil de Biedma from the effects of AIDS, but that of Rock Hudson that drew publicity. Information failed to produce awareness: there was a wave of national hysteria against children with AIDS, who were expelled from schools (p. 149).

Education was not targeted to gays because of the 'absurd belief' that they suffered no discrimination in the social democratic state and thus required no special treatment (p. 150). If AIDS was closeted it was because of an exaggerated respect for the privacy of gay men, who, lacking existence as a social group, were deprived of both information and representation. Ironically, when Telemadrid broadcast a news programme characteristically entitled 'The Other Face of AIDS' (1 December 1992), drug users appeared as such; gays did not in any guise recognizable to the TV audience, a situation with which the Spanish media were happy to collude (pp. 151–2). Likewise when Almodóvar appeared on national Antena 3's 'Queremos saber' (We want to know), he insisted that public figures should not be expected to reveal their HIV status, when to be positive meant to be treated as a plague carrier. For Mira however, this is to neglect the public figure's ethical responsibility and social commitment: while grief is properly private, AIDS is a public affair (pp. 153–4). The problem of the discontinuity of Spanish AIDS education is also, then, a problem of visibility: as long as official policy persists in claiming that there is no homophobia (or racism) in Spain, then homosexuals (or blacks) cannot appear as such, deprived as they are of any image repertoire which might give specific meaning or context to their existence independent of that of other citizens (p. 161).

The second area which may sound familiar to English-speakers is José Miguel G. Cortés's account of AIDS activism in Spain, heavily dependent as it is on North American precedents. Although Cortés begins with a dense account of the 'social construction of external reality which is transformed in respect to itself and to the structure of individual thought' (pp. 93–4), his critique of the vagueness and ambiguity of public health authority poster campaigns in Spain is trenchant (p. 99). In contrast, the efforts of small and courageous activist groups in Madrid, Barcelona and Valencia offer simple and direct warnings to those unaddressed by the government: that AIDS kills women;[23] that syringes should be cleaned with bleach (p. 102). Cortés also recounts direct actions against the university and newspapers of Valencia and a poster campaign against Jordi Pujol (leader of the Catalan autonomous government) whose graphic style is reminiscent of Gran Fury's attacks on Reagan and New York Mayor Koch (p. 105). Cortés ends by lamenting the paucity and poverty of groups such as the Barcelonan ACTUA, citing the disproportion between the high incidence of AIDS in Spain and the low level of response to it (p. 108).

Another, much longer piece by Cortés in the collection, however, strikes quite a different note. 'On Death and Dying' begins with an argument (also shared by Baudrillard) that modernity and rationalism are founded on the exclusion of death from the social sphere. Tracing, after Philippe Ariès, the progressive disappearance of the dying and the dead, Cortés notes how funerals, tombs and cemeteries have been progressively 'devisualized' (p. 41), as religion has handed death over to medicine, exiled it to the hospital and rendered it 'pure negativity' (p. 45). The task today is to 'incorporate death into daily existence' and reverse the conception of death and sickness as alien to the subject. Only then can we strip the corpse of its current 'absolute passivity' and address it as a reminder of temporality, carnality and putrefaction (p. 47). Punning on *escatología* (both scatology and eschatology in Spanish), Cortés perceives the confrontation with the horror of death as a form of ultimate knowledge in US artists such as Cindy Sherman and Robert Mapplethorpe and lesser-known Spaniards such as Frederic Amat, whose *Anatomía* presents us with a body without skin, limbs or organs, a body of congealed or arrested blood (p. 60). AIDS would thus be an intensification of that daily (but repressed) double connection between our relation to the body (of life and death) and assumption of death as just another part of everyday existence (p. 62).

The parallel with Baudrillard's fatal strategies is obvious, even if the language is less ecstatic, more pragmatic. Setting death against death ('combating obscenity with its own weapons'), Cortés and Amat propose we incorporate fatality as a cure for a wounded symbolic and social order. And in the one piece devoted entirely to literature in *De amor y rabia*,[24] critic and novelist Vicente Molina Foix appeals to Baudrillard's principle of evil in order to read the works of AIDS: 'the principle of Evil is not moral, it is a principle of disequilibrium and of vertigo, a principle of complexity and strangeness, a principle of incompatibility, of antagonism, and irreducibility' (p. 313). As disarticulation (*déliaison, desligamiento*), Baudrillard's evil is thus a vital principle. Like Artaud's theatre of the plague (also cited at length by Molina), it tends to disrupt the banalities of naturalism and the everyday with the pure gesturality of convulsive beauty (p. 298). Stressing the organicity of the thinking subject (most particularly in relation to the autobiographical fictions of Hervé Guibert), Molina contrasts the quantity and quality of English- and French-language narratives of AIDS with the single Spanish volume known to him at the time of writing (1990), a vengeful, moralistic and pseudonymous science fiction mystery called, characteristically, *Proyecto Venus Letal* (The Lethal Venus Project) (p. 308).

I shall return to science fiction when I discuss Eduardo Haro Ibars below. But first we should examine the one major essayist of AIDS in Spain, Alberto Cardín, to whom Cortés dedicates a chapter in his anthology.[25] Cortés begins with the paradox that despite the high incidence of the epidemic in Spain, the generally liberal cultural climate and the large number of gay artists and intellectuals, there is an almost complete absence of response to the epidemic. Although it is decimating a generation and is being exploited by the agents of reaction in Spain, those most affected by AIDS have enlisted neither in the activist struggle for solidarity and survival, nor in the ideological struggle against the New Right (p. 167). Unlike others such as Haro Ibars, Gil de Biedma and Néstor Almendros, Cardín openly proclaimed his HIV status in 1985, and is the editor of two collections on the syndrome: the unfortunately titled *SIDA: ¿Maldición bíblica o enfermedad letal?* (AIDS: Biblical Curse or Lethal Illness?, 1985) and *SIDA: Enfoques alternativos* (AIDS: Alternative Approaches, 1991). In the introduction to the first, Cardín gives an account, at once personal and general, of the inadequate medical response to AIDS in Spain and castigates Spanish gays for their lack of awareness or commitment (*concienciación*): their multiple partners, indifference to others and ignorance. Cardín proposes an ethics of the subject in its deployment of the body, which sets the individual's choice of self-destruction in the pursuit of private pleasure against the state's putative right to intervene to preserve the life of its citizens. The second book argues for a transformation of the sick person from the passive agent of medical expertise into the subject of his or her illness, and stresses the importance of 'self-love' (pp. 170–1).

This coinage leads back to an extended essay more appropriate to our theme here: *Lo próximo y lo ajeno* (Self and Other, 1990), a work which (according to Cortés) was wholly ignored by the academic and cultural establishment on its publication. A sociological and anthropological critique of 'gay identity', this essay strikes a Deleuzian anti-liberation note, denying that homosexuality can be a 'way of being' in which a self is realized through sex (p. 173). It thus follows, however, that if it is indeed the case that a putative gay culture in Spain is tied to specific sexual practices, then any change in those practices will force a revolution in the fabric of a fragile and provisional identity which requires constant external reinforcement in order to prop itself up (p. 173). What is needed, then, is a change in the conception of the body as a simple instrument of pleasure and an acceptance of coexistence with a body that is vulnerable, wounded and suffering (p. 174). Cardín predicts the disappearance of existing gay culture in Spain, based as it is on unsymbolized private pleasures. The challenge of AIDS is thus the production of new forms of relation between self and other (of solidarity, understanding and affect), new forms which will address both physical trauma and existential self-interrogation.

Ironically, Cardín's prediction of the death of homosexuality echoes that of French theorist Guy Hocquenghem some twenty years earlier.[26] But where Hocquenghem argued that a Deleuzian critique of the violent imposition of sexual identity would lead to a multiplication of sexual activities, Cardín argues to the contrary that the excessive reliance of sexual identity on sexual activity renders that identity spurious or precarious when activities are obliged to change in frequency or form. But in his respect for, in his love of, the mortally wounded body, Cardín repeats that gesture of incorporation (of the remainder, of death) which we have seen in other Spanish intellectuals. Moreover, in the virulence of his polemic and his insistence on the organicity of the writing subject (typical of his work as a whole), Cardín comes close to the fatal strategy of ecstatic simulation or seduction.

For example, *Como si nada* (All the Same),[27] an essay written before Cardín's engagement with AIDS and thus necessarily un-examined by Cortés, combines the highest level of theoretical complexity with the most relentless critique of the Spanish media and intellectual establishment. Claiming he resorts to bulimia or masturbation in order to gain the peace of mind he requires to think, that he gives himself up to bouts of writing that are 'convulsive' (pp. 14, 81), Cardín also proposes a Nietzschean and Lacanian theory of subjectivity in which 'the voice of the body cures' (p. 37) while, nevertheless, the subject stands perplexed before the object that is its own body (p. 60). If, for Cardín, writing originates in a 'narcissistic wound' (p. 75), then this is because it simply reproduces that repeated attempt by the ego to shore itself up against the void by incorporating that object which it has itself set up as a decoy for its wounds (p. 77). However, if the ego is but the residue of these multiple resistances, if the body is but a garment with no absolute nakedness possible (pp. 76, 71), then the self is wholly reified, 'as false and defenceless as an idol taken down from its pedestal' (p. 71).

Cardín's general critique of subjectivity and agency thus points forward to his more specific attack on gay identity, on its wounds and its lures. However, Cardín's political crusade against the Spanish critical and medical establishment and his ethical engagement with the body of the other are (as he knows full well) undermined by his equally intransigent stress on the embodiment of writing and his insistence on an unconscious which (citing Lacan) 'never ceases to be written' (p. 84). It would be crass to dwell on the bodily figures of Cardín's pre-AIDS essays, as if they somehow anticipated his subsequent illness: Cardín himself satirized the 'strange fascination' felt by 'vulgar journalists' for 'the [dead] bodies of homosexual poets', such as Lorca and Barthes (p. xxxvi). More important is to stress that his ethical and political commitment, readily recognizable to an Anglo-American reader-ship, is shot through with a less familiar and more disquieting disequilibrium or movement to extremes proper to the fatal strategy, a spiral of dislocation in which theory becomes 'a parade of private monsters, composed of scraps of the self' (p. 18).

That parade of monsters, that movement from the aesthetic to the ecstatic, is much more explicit in my second figure, Eduardo Haro Ibars. In *De amor y rabia* Haro appears only in monstrous, cadaverous form: in his regular column in the national daily *El Mundo* (28 December 1992), gay poet and novelist Luis Antonio de Villena recounts how he once saw the ailing Haro arrive at the ballet: 'extravagantly garbed, decrepit, and made-up' (p. 265). Villena avoided his one-time friend, fearful of having to give him a social kiss. Now repentant, Villena claims that the true horror of AIDS is not the ravages it wreaks on young men such as Haro; rather it is reactions such as his own, of timorous and shameful rejection. Ironically, however, Haro (author in the 1970s of a seminal study of *Gay Rock*[28]) is, in his post-AIDS fiction at least, hardly squeamish about the grotesque and the decrepit. On the contrary his last novel *Intersecciones*[29] mixes corporality, liquidity and putrefaction to produce a heady brew indeed.

The setting of *Intersecciones* is an apocalyptic, post-plague city, clearly based on Madrid. As Inquisitional bonfires burn, ghostly inhabitants gamble with gold teeth by the light of lamp shades made of human skin (p. 11). In this collapsed chronology ('We should rub out the calendars'), the monsters and the sick are eradicated in a final 'Autumn Sale': the new end of the world (p. 12). Shreds of skin, smoke and charred gums advance along the gas-lit avenues (p. 13). While these remainders of the body are persistent, there is no doubt as to the cause of their abjection. Nightclubs are lit by the small light of a corpse and nocturnal vultures worship the deity whose secret name is Putrefaction (p. 14). And there 'we' are, inhaling the perfume of fields of sperm at nightfall, propping up bars where we plant a kiss on the Beast's entrails, or venturing out to Mengele's hairdressing salon to procure the skin disease treatment needed by 'mummies' such as ourselves (p. 15).

Haro savours the typically Burroughsian metamorphoses of the body, stripped of the sensual luxury of flesh: now cloaked with scaly skin, now dissolving into promiscuously mixed fluids (p. 38). But the most transparent and perhaps most successful of Haro's fatal strategies is the section entitled 'The elegance of matter destined for the tomb'. The Sad Duke named La Látigo (Lady Whip) enumerates the aesthetic pleasures of death: the garlands of worms and flesh; the final necklaces made of our own tiny bones; a gilded and scarlet sunset complementing the beauty of putrefaction to be found in gangrene – greens, blues, silken splendours and frost-blasted foliage, forests of moss flourishing in open wounds (p. 40). Beneath the skin of grotesquely swollen fairies lies 'a terrible, poisonous truth', where half-formed larvae attract unsuspecting men with 'a fantastic and deceitful appearance of beauty' (p. 41). But this horror is not only associated with a phantasmic homosexuality; it is quite explicitly anal and oral: extinct creatures once engaged in bizarre copulation with a Black Hole; beasts of the boudoir will willingly suck you with toothless gums (pp. 42–3).

But if the scene is fantastic, it is also strangely familiar. The 'insect disease' supposedly transmitted by mosquitoes takes some five years to incubate (p. 47); the Obscure Theocrat is the now forgotten Franco (p. 49); and the cruising ground of Madrid's Casa de Campo, in whose amusement park Haro's replicants of the wild boys play, retains its own name (p. 59). What is disturbing, then, about *Intersecciones* is not simply its extremes of fantasy (in which it promotes in Baudrillardian style the falser than false, the uglier than ugly); it is the interruption of that fantastic register by moments of unambiguous historical reference. Moving ever towards extremes, exhausting its narrative in an intensifying spiral, *Intersecciones* also, and more disturbingly, advances its fatal strategy by combining grotesque mimicry and simple repetition in an uneasy symbiosis. Haro's narrator announces that decadence came with the invention of the 'duplicator', a machine for replicating ideas, objects and even people (p. 51). Likewise, the work of his narrative is like the action of Baudrillard's ecstatic simulation, annihilating the difference between original and copy.

For Haro, himself stigmatized by Villena as the grotesque ghost of the ballet, the body dwindles into a dislocated remainder: scraps of flesh and skin blown along the grand avenues; blood and lymph coagulated in the wake of frightful orgies. But in the tradition of his chosen genre, the body is also prosthesis: supplemented by cyborg technology, imprinted on 'memory circuits' (p. 75). While Cardín the essayist seeks in AIDS a new relation to the other (a relation he problematizes by the subtlety of his theory and the cruelty of his polemic), Haro the novelist finds in AIDS a fantasy of the body's inability to distinguish itself from the other, to reemerge from a final fusion of blood and sperm. But Haro does not preclude, even in extremis, the space for personal reference: the ancient hero named Alberto, whose very 'remains' (*despojos*) have now disappeared (p. 53), is eerily reminiscent of the Alberto Cardín who was the author of a volume of verse also called *Despojos*.[30] It is a particularizing reference that would not be permitted by the hermetic and abstract conceptualism of Pepe Espaliú.

3. 'FOR THOSE WHO NO LONGER LIVE IN ME':
PEPE ESPALIÚ

As Juan Vicente Aliaga, his most authoritative commentator, notes, the approach to Pepe Espaliú is always problematic.[31] There is little doubt that Espaliú is the Spanish artist, essayist and intellectual whose intervention in the AIDS epidemic has been most effective and carries greatest moral authority; yet his mature work is highly elusive and enigmatic, derived from a conceptualist tradition which is barely accessible to non-initiates. There is thus considerable debate both inside and outside Spain as to the nature and validity of his work. On the one hand, two of his pieces ('El nido' [The Nest] and 'Carrying') have been chosen by critics as amongst the most representative of Spanish art of the last twenty years;[32] on the other, a Spanish newspaper could write on the occasion of the posthumous retrospective at the Reina Sofía that Espaliú was 'known more for his activism against the pandemic than for his achievements as an artist'.[33] Or again, while Espaliú argued repeatedly in interviews that Spain needed people who could speak directly ('sin rodeos') (for example, *De amor*, p. 136), his work itself was characterized by indirection and indeed circularity, a circularity which (for Aliaga) relates both to a desire trapped in repeated, pulsional movements and a motion of support, of 'love in solidarity' (*De amor*, p. 78). Hence, while the catalogue of Espaliú's 1994 exhibition at the Institute of Contemporary Arts in London begins by citing critic José Luis Brea's statement: 'Nobody can ever have doubted what Pepe Espaliú was talking about',[34] the catalogue to the official exhibition of Spanish art at the Seville Expo of 1992 cites Espaliú himself on 'images which can talk only in silence'.[35] A British review of the ICA show claims that Espaliú was 'too scared' to face up to his predicament, 'skirt[ing] around his personal and mortal dilemmas'.[36] In Spain, however, where differing definitions of privacy meant that Espaliú was more likely to be criticized for being too outspoken than too reticent, the catalogue to the Reina Sofía show praises the artist for his sense of subjectivity as an 'intimate connection' between artistic production and existential incident. Beyond simple individualism or banal allegory, Espaliú's works form 'a hinge between the constellation of the external world and our own internal spaces'.[37]

Manel Clot's essay from which I take these words is called 'Two

Words on Love (An Idea of Disaster)'. And I would argue myself that Espaliú's work enacts in the visual arts both the ethics of alterity and the ecstasy of eschatology which we have seen in representations of AIDS by Spanish writers. Moreover, like a figure such as Cardín once more, Espaliú is deeply influenced by psychoanalysis, and indeed attended Lacan's seminar in Paris. It thus follows that he approaches the problem of the subject and the problem of reference obliquely and with some deliberation. And if Espaliú's fatal strategy of the object (which is always vertiginous, complex and irreducible) is less apocalyptic than, say, that of Haro, it is no less final or definitive. Straining to hear the mute speech of the body, to see the invisible intersection of the somatic and the social, Espaliú explores those figures in which the organic remainder reminds us of our being-in-the-world (such as the nest) or in which the inorganic prosthesis points to the breaching of the body and the possibility of solidarity (such as the crutch). It is a project which is at once aesthetic, intellectual and political.

Juan Vicente Aliaga has stressed this secret flow of diverse themes using the impeccably Lacanian topos of the knot: combining the threads of circularity and sex, of illness and dispossession, of concealment, identity and the body, Espaliú marks or remarks a knot (or circumference) without beginning or end ('Speak to Me, Body', p. 146). And a sense of plurality is clear in a series of related works from the late 1980s in bronze and leather or on paper and cardboard which figure resolutely secret or monstrous objects.[38] Thus the 'Pinochio' (sic) series on cardboard (1988) shows a number of masks flattened, pierced or sewn, mimicking in their shape bodily organs such as the heart; or the mixed-media and punningly titled 'Pas de masque' duplicates dressmaking patterns which remain, however, unrelated to any bodily parts they might clothe. Untitled mixed-media constructs of the same year are reminiscent of flu masks or jockstraps, pierced and sewn once more and mounted as enigmatic trophies on wooden bases. The four 'Santos' pieces of 1989 (crafted from leather in Espaliú's native Córdoba) resemble saddles, shoes, masks and sex toys, their brown leather ironically alluding to human skin. While the paper works play with surface and depth (through shading or the grafting on to organic forms of the paper flaps typical of cut-out dolls' clothing), the three-dimensional works explore the relation between volume and cavity: just as mask and face are indistinguishable, so body part and supplement are inseparable. Espaliú's prostheses are thus simulacra in Baudrillard's definition of the term: copies for which no original (no bodily organ or limb) remains (Plate 12).

Espaliú develops this critique of the body in a recurrent motif of his late work, the tortoise shell. At once prosthesis and remainder (supplement to the living being, remnant of the dead), the shell substitutes for the human head in an untitled drawing on paper (1989); or, cast in ominous bronze, is suspended vertically over a prone organic form, placed on the floor beneath it ('Untitled', 1989). A bronze shell and a coil of knotted rope placed side by side on a two-legged table ('Untitled', also 1989) juxtapose and imply a relation between hermetic enclosure and flexible virtuality. The rope returns in an untitled bronze of 1990: a schematic, head-less torso is surmounted by two skipping ropes hanging from its 'shoulders', simulating legs or arms. Just as a fetish object (mask or jockstrap) substitutes for that symbolic castration it at once asserts and denies, so the prosthesis at once stands in for the 'proper' part of the body and improperly outstrips it, acquiring a resonant, symbolic power which the organic, naturalistic figure is denied.

Allegories with no patent solution, abstractions with no fixed referent, Espaliú's objects resolutely remain material comments on the desolation of the body and the social insolidarity provoked by AIDS, which (as Aliaga has observed) took Espaliú not to the margins of experience but rather to its very centre ('Speak to Me, Body', p. 154). More specifically, Espaliú's enigmatic objects can be seen as ghostly figures of the fatal strategy. In Espaliú's shows we sense, as in Baudrillard's vision of Pompeii, a 'freezing of time . . . in the fossilised and fugitive signs of everyday existence . . . the perfect simulacrum of our own death'. The significance of suspension then (of Espaliú's placing of heavy bronzes above the spectators' heads) is to evoke catastrophe: 'stopping things before they come to an end, and holding them suspended in their apparition' ('Fatal Strategies', p. 197). In such conditions, the old illusionism can no longer work. In the fatal strategy the object displaces the subject (the shell the head): 'An objective irony watches over us, it is the object's fulfilment without regard for the subject, nor for its alienation' (p. 198); or again: 'the object . . . as opposed to the subject . . . is a bad conductor of the symbolic order, yet a good conductor of the fatal, that is, of pure objectivity, sovereign and irreconcilable, immanent and enigmatic' (p. 199).

Hermetic and self-sufficient, suspended mute in their irony, Espaliú's objects speak nonetheless (like Baudrillard's theory) of the dereliction of the social sphere, which can no longer be imaged directly or reduced to simple symbolic equivalence.

In an important collection of prose fragments Espaliú has sketched out a project reminiscent of Baudrillard's, addressing 'those who see in night not the negation of light, but rather light in its most extreme form; light opposing itself to light, light transfigured into light as only reality, full and empty of itself.'[39] For Espaliú, 'the opposite of vision is not the invisible, but the palpable: light delivered over to touch, light made body, the link or ligament between body and eye' (p. 53). Rejecting with Baudrillard, then, the dialectic of meaning and moving with him to extremes, Espaliú also proposes vision as 'a wound traced in the depths of one's being [intimidad]; the knowledge that while you look out of yourself, others are looking at you. Eye dilating in the darkness, . . . naked pupil of the madman, of the drug addict, of the maniac and the pervert' (p. 51).

The desolation of the remainder and the rupture of the prosthesis do not, then, provoke humanist pathos. Rather, in their very negativity, they incite a new mode of representation (a link between body and eye) and a new ethics of solidarity (with the madman, the drug addict and the pervert). And Espaliú's last works retain the earlier sense of disequilibrium and vertigo, of complexity and strangeness, while addressing from that same dazzling darkness a new ethics of the relation between self and other, based on the incorporation of death into life. This sense of ethics is exemplified by the iron work 'Para los que ya no viven en mí' (For those who no longer live in me, 1992): two arc- or tomb-shaped boxes attached to the wall, the right hermetically sealed, the left enclosed by a tight-fitting metal cage (Plate 13). The mute but knowing repetition of the piece both marks and memorializes the definitive singularity of death (doubly insulated and internalized) and the insufficiency of the single subject (its continuing penetration by others who live, or once lived, in it).

This is also an aspect of one of Espaliú's most resonant figures: the sedan chair. A repeated series of sealed boxes with schematic supports in iron ('Carrying I', 1992) traverse false walls at impossible angles, suspended above or below the spectator (Plate 14). Like the fetish object the sedan chair mimics the form of the human body. Unlike it, it suggests movement rather than the frozen moment of desire and intersubjectivity rather than the singular evolution of a psyche. But if the sedan chair is motion and solidarity, it is also (in Espaliú's treatment) seclusion and quarantine. For Aliaga it invokes the hospital stretcher and the risk of contagion (p. 154). Yet in this resonant and discreet social reference Espaliú is also at his most aesthetically rigorous, combining (as Aliaga notes once more) a 'mutating, unstable, deceptive representational space' with the balance and rhythm of classicism (p. 156).

The fusion or confusion of the aesthetic and the social is equally apparent in the performance or action also known as 'Carrying' which took place in San Sebastián and Madrid in 1992. A barefoot and bedraggled Espaliú was transported along a prepared route by successive pairs of (quite literal) supporters who linked hands beneath him (Plate 15). Here Espaliú, who had recently returned from New York, created an indigenous activist event, which received considerable media coverage (Almodóvar and Bibi Andersen were amongst the participants in Madrid) and which was later spontaneously imitated elsewhere in Spain. But typically that indigenous form, less literalist and more metaphoric than its US equivalents, was itself inspired by crosscultural and bilingual confusion: Espaliú had noticed how Latino buddies whose grasp of English was none too sure seemed to collapse 'caring' and 'carrying'. It was a specific linguistic lapse, which brought with it its unavoidable reference to the particular conditions and terminology of the New York AIDS crisis, including the English idiom 'AIDS carrier', which lent Espaliú the opportunity for his intervention in Spain as artist and as activist. Eschewing what he felt to be propaganda and the tradition of 'social artists' in Spain with their very limited audience, Espaliú thus achieved a performance that was at once widely diffused and resolutely complex, employing, as Aliaga notes, 'successive levels of visual symbolism that gradually become interconnected' (p. 156). And the mode of argument here (as in the fatal strategy) is not dialectical, but paradoxical: taking to extremes that fragility of the body, those practices of exclusion and scapegoating (Aliaga, p. 157) which society has violently imposed on PWAs who dare to be visible, Espaliú heightened that vulnerability, barefoot and bare-headed in driving rain, adopting a modestly Christ-like posture: borne along by his supporters in a new, queer Deposition.

The subsequent piece 'El nido' (The Nest, inexplicably mistranslated as The Neck in English-language catalogues and commentaries) also combined (in Aliaga's words) density of meaning with formal concision (p. 147). Performed at the Sonsbeek Festival in 1993 on seven successive days, it consisted of a formally dressed Espaliú circling a platform placed high in a tree and removing a piece of clothing on each circuit until, naked, he climbed back down a ladder to earth (Plate 16). In the video record of the performance, Espaliú occasionally pauses and regards the discarded garments beneath his feet or the hidden spectator (watching from the gallery window). The piece is, however, wholly devoid of narcissism or exhibitionism. The pathos of the figure, slightly paunchy as it is and with skinny legs, would seem at first to bear out Simon Grant's contention that here Espaliú is referring not to *the* body, but to *his* body.[40] The problem with this personalized reading, however, is that it neglects the varied and communal contexts in which the piece is inscribed. These would include ecology (with Espaliú repeatedly divesting himself of his covering, as a bird does its feathers); psychoanalysis (the body as function of the remnants it expels: urine and semen); and politics (the endless circling of prisoners at recreation). All of these contexts are suggested by Espaliú in his texts and examined by Aliaga in his commentary. Moreover, Espaliú in the performance made an unusually explicit reference: stamping the paper around the circumference of the tree with the phrase (in English): 'AIDS is around'. As in 'Carrying' the cross-linguistic pun (supplemented here by citing Emily Dickinson's 'My business is circumference') has a force which is at once ironic and iconic. The Espaliú who protested against euphemistic or periphrastic language ('hablar por rodeos') here performs a compulsively repeated circularity, one which is now, however, at once pathetic and positive, the expression of a commitment that is simultaneously theoretical and political.

The circularity of form, the compulsive repetition of desire and the insistence of political intervention are seen in an event contemporary with 'El nido': Espaliú invited four gay men to meet in a *vespasienne* (circular Parisian pissoir). After scrawling graffiti on the walls, they were to assemble in a nearby hotel and reveal their identities to each other. While the aesthetic, psychoanalytic and social concerns of this piece fall squarely within the confines of Espaliú's earlier work, it shares a wilful and defiant explicitness (a vindication of the round dance of queer partnering which many moralists hoped AIDS would bring to an end) with another of Espaliú's last works, an untitled collage on paper (1993). The top half consists of a found image (rare in Espaliú's work): a photograph in extreme close-up of an erect penis and hand just after orgasm, the scrotum apparently pierced by nails. The bottom half reveals a delicately shaded drawing of a form which bulges towards the bottom: an inverted flower, wine glass or penis once more. While this piece is reproduced in the catalogue of the large retrospective of Espaliú curated by Aliaga and subsidized by the regional government (Junta) of Espaliú's native Andalucía, it was not shown amongst Espaliú's last works at the Reina Sofía in Madrid, arousing accusations of censorship. A come shot might seem to be the dramatic culmination of Espaliú's persistent working through the body over a decade of artistic production. But, as Aliaga reminds us, explicitness is no guarantee of ease of interpretation: how are we to read the dislocation between the photograph and drawing that are juxtaposed without explanation (p. 152)? Aliaga does, however, associate the image with an Anglo-American style coming out, in conjunction with a late autobiographical text by Espaliú which claims that homosexuality is equivalent to a definitive exclusion from the social, juridical, religious, political and economic spheres. Aliaga continues:

> In a country of silences like Spain, where, behind apparent tolerance, the rights of the gay and lesbian community are trampled underfoot, public recognition of homosexuality meant, for Espaliú, ceasing to live his art as a fictitious construction, as an alibi when facing up to the problems of everyday life . . . in terms of reality (if not of realism). (p. 153)

The final parenthesis is important here. For if Espaliú may have come to experience his life in terms of truth and falsity (of face and mask, light and dark), then, as we have seen, his work, to the very end, ceaselessly problematizes that dialectic, choosing rather the paradoxes of the fatal strategy and working through to a darkness which is not the opposite of light, but rather its greatest intensity. The image which remains with me of the late Espaliú is not the ejaculating penis (however subtly qualified by the delicate graphic tracery beneath it) but rather the series of painted iron crutches known as 'Paseo del amigo' (The Friend's

Walk, 1993). Pastel-coloured and apparently inoffensive, they recline enigmatically against the wall in threes; assume a tiered, descending formation above the floor (no. II); or, in another piece called 'El nido', link arm rests to form an unbroken circle (Plate 17). Hermetic, abstracted and ominous (wholly independent of the bodies they were once intended to support), still they gesture mutely to the possibility of solidarity, to a breach in that mortal exclusion and isolation which Espaliú (like Cardín) held to be the position of gay men and PWAs in Spain.

4. THE LOOK OF AIDS

A press photo of the opening of Espaliú's posthumous retrospective in Madrid shows the then director of the Reina Sofía, María Corral, posing with one of the works on display: 'Rumi' of 1993 (Plate 18). Elegantly coiffed and couture-clad, clutching her catalogue, she stares out from behind Espaliú's massive and menacing iron piece: four interconnected iron bird cages descending diagonally from the ceiling.[41] In its play on inside and outside, containment and display, the photo not only captures that fusion of the conceptual and the political typical of Espaliú's late work, but also points up the problematic placing of that work within the arts policy of the Spanish state. Corral was later dismissed by Minister of Culture Carmen Alborch, allegedly for failing to devote enough of the centre's resources to the promotion of native Spanish artists such as Espaliú.

The director posing with the cage: writers such as Cardín or Haro, less dependent than visual artists on state sponsorship, could hardly complain of such incorporation by a benign Socialist autocracy. Indeed, their work was ignored by the national press.[42] But if Espaliú's challenging and disturbing project was indeed assimilated by the Spanish cultural establishment (a simultaneous one-man show in London formed part of an officially sponsored Spanish arts festival in the UK), then this need not mean that its political import was wholly erased. Indeed, I have argued that just as the academic and art activists of *De amor y rabia* move from political commitment to cultural theory, so Espaliú himself evolved from conceptual minimalism to overt activism, without, however, abandoning that layering of conceptual strata, that interweaving of aesthetic knots or circles, that distinguished his work throughout his career.

If, then, Spanish theory and abstraction are more political than they might at first appear (embodied as they are in the paradoxes of the fatal strategy), then Anglo-American art activism is more theoretical, less unmediated, than might at first be supposed. Douglas Crimp places Gran Fury and other AIDS collectives firmly within the context of a postmodern art practice that 'deliberately complicated the notion of "the artist"' and addressed 'questions of identity, authorship, and audience – and the ways in which all three are constructed through representation' (*AIDS Demo Graphics*, p. 18). Hence, far from simply asserting a pre-existing identity or community in its wholly justified and righteous rage, New York AIDS art activists problematized the subject (of art, of illness) in their conviction that 'identity . . . is coercively imposed by perceived sexual orientation or HIV status [and] . . . at the same time, wilfully taken on, in defiant declaration of affinity with the "others" of AIDS: queers, women, Blacks, Latinos, drug users, sex workers.' In a very different social and medical context, and much more explicitly engaged with a psychoanalytic and philo-sophical critique of identity, artists and intellectuals of the Spanish state also worked towards a solidarity with the other, one which they believed could not be achieved, however, without a rigorous critique of representation itself.

As the multiple members of Gran Fury concealed their identity behind a collective and ironically reappropriated name,[43] so Espaliú staged the impersonality of the artist in the smooth, blank surfaces of his bronze and iron sculptures, and Haro, in a very different way, celebrated the dissolution of the individual body in the abject putrefaction of flesh. Theirs is, in Baudrillard's phrase, an 'ironic art of disappearance' which 'succeed[s] the art of survival' (p. 203). Living on, even the acerbic and idiosyn-cratic Cardín dissolves his ego into an endlessly reflexive play of mirrored objects. My initial hypothesis for the unique ravages of AIDS in Spain is thus insufficient: a disabused awareness of the paradoxes of identity and visibility did not prevent North Americans from producing a rich variety of artistic responses to the epidemic; inversely, the Spanish state has recently enjoyed a rebirth of lesbian and gay activism in which signs of community (dedicated book shops, lobby groups, extensive press coverage) have for the first time become defiantly and confidently overt.[44] Even a celebration of camp stereotypes such as Leopoldo Alas's *La acera de enfrente* [Up Queer Street] ends with its malicious and prancing queens enlisting with a thinly veiled version of the newly reformed activist group COGAM (Comunidad Gay de Madrid).[45] There is thus no reason to suppose that Spain is inherently resistant to notions of gay identity or community; indeed, the Spanish Constitution of 1978 has proved one of the most fruitful legislative fields in Europe for the putting into practice of the European Parliament's 1994 resolution on homosexual equality.

The Spanish state (and most particularly the Basque Country and Valencia) are thus pioneers in the development of 'new loves, new families',[46] and in the legal protection of same-sex partnerships and parenting.[47] But perhaps there are indeed historical causes for the silence and invisibility of AIDS in Spain, which become ever more troubling. In a round-table discussion by artists in *De amor y rabia*, participants relate the evolution of resistance under Franco to a certain democratic deficit under the Socialists: during the dictatorship, dissent could not be individual, but was rather highly organized with 'the Party assum[ing] the sense of the people' (p. 124). And since revolutionary struggle was channelled through a 'monolithic' Left political structure (p. 123), then problems would inevitably be delegated to the appropriate representatives. While PWAs in the US felt obliged in the absence of social welfare structures to assume individual responsibilities, in a Spain which now enjoyed free and universal health care, there was no tradition of forming self-protection groups, pragmatically centred on single issues.[48] It is not or not simply then (as one artist argues) that US sexual repression led to activism while European tolerance worked against it; it is rather that the representative democracy enjoyed by Spain, and the long, clandestine opposition which preceded it, have tended inadvertently but definitively to distance citizens from the public sphere and to delay the representation of new issues or communities in that sphere.

Baudrillard warns chillingly: 'It is in the full light of day that certain things come to their designated end' (p. 203). In their critique of representation (whether political or artistic) Spanish artists and intellectuals question that 'becoming visible' which is so brutally enacted in the 'look of AIDS'. But in their appeal to the fatal strategy they propose a dangerous and ambitious response to that dereliction or abjection of the body. Their moral is that which Adrian Searle found in Espaliú's performance of 'El nido', in which the artist repeatedly divested himself of his clothes. It is that 'a loss one has already suffered might be made up for by a loss one brings on oneself' ('The Loss of Pepe Espaliú', p. 23). As we have seen, Spaniards have argued that amongst the losses of AIDS is that of death, whose exile from representation has led to a 'loss of symbolic value in culture'. The reincorporation of death is by no means an inviting project at a time of such profligate and pointless human loss. For Spanish artists and intellectuals, however, it is a fatal strategy which is not only indispensable if their nation is finally to address the pandemic; it is also (as it is for Baudrillard) a vital weapon in the battle to restore to an ailing body politic the rich resources of a symbolic exchange which are so urgently required to revitalize the public sphere.

NOTES

1   See Jonathan Mann et al., eds, *AIDS in the World* (Cambridge, MA and London: Harvard University Press, 1992), pp. 47, 83, 116, 709; and Jesús M. de Miguel and David L. Kirp, 'Spain: An Epidemic of Denial', in David L. Kirp and Ronald Bayer, eds, *AIDS in the Industrialized Democracies* (New Brunswick: Rutgers University Press, 1992), pp. 168–84.

2   Ricardo Lorenzo and Héctor Anabitarte, 'Un día en el gueto y sin hablar del SIDA', in *SIDA: el asunto está que arde* (Madrid: Revolución, 1987), pp. 89–99.

3   Jeffrey Weeks, 'AIDS: The Intellectual Agenda', in Peter Aggleton et al., eds, *AIDS: Social Representations, Social Practices* (New York: Falmer, 1989), p. 11.

4   The Spanish press has consistently failed to name AIDS as a cause of the death of public figures. Where it is reported, as in the case of fashion designer Manuel Piña, the rhetoric of 'AIDS victim' is still used and a photo of the proud and handsome subject is pruriently captioned 'Manuel Piña, months before disease affected his face'; see Luis Navarrete, 'Muere el diseñador Manuel Piña, víctima del SIDA', *El País* (9 October 1994).

5   Deborah Lupton, *Moral Threats and Dangerous Desires: AIDS in the News Media* (London: Taylor & Francis, 1994), p. 117.

6   Sander Gilman, 'Plague in Germany 1939/1989: Cultural Images of Race, Space, and Disease', in Timothy F. Murphy and Suzanne Poirier, eds, *Writing AIDS: Gay Literature, Language, and Analysis* (New York: Columbia University Press, 1993), p. 54.

7   Simon Watney, 'The Subject of AIDS', in Aggleton et al., *AIDS: Social Representations*, p. 70.

8   Juan Vicente Aliaga and José Miguel G. Cortés, *De amor y rabia: acerca del arte y el SIDA* (Valencia: Universidad Politécnica de Valencia, 1993). My

thanks to Juan Vicente Aliaga for kindly providing me with a copy of this book.

9 Jean Baudrillard, 'Fatal Strategies', in Mark Poster, ed., *Selected Writings* (Cambridge: Polity, 1988), p. 206.

10 'The Subject of AIDS', p. 72.

11 *De amor y rabia*, p. 136.

12 Cindy Patton, 'Inventing African AIDS', in *Inventing AIDS* (New York and London: Routledge, 1990), pp. 77–97.

13 Recent official figures from the Ministerio de Sanidad are reported in *Entiendes* 30 (May 1994), p. 51. They give a total of 24,202 PWAs at 31 March 1994; and claim that 'drug addiction' accounts for 64 per cent of cases of transmission, 'homosexual males' 15 per cent. A note in the same issue reports that the Plan Nacional del SIDA, for which the Ministry is responsible, was without a director for four months in 1993–94 (p. 53).

14 Official and academic studies, which still distinguish between the 'general public' and 'risk groups', would hardly encourage men to identify themselves as gay to researchers; see the report published in Madrid by the Ministerio de Salud y Consumo (Plan Nacional sobre el SIDA): *Actitudes sociales ante el SIDA: informe de resultados, población general* (1990); and Ricardo Usieto Atondo, *Anomía y marginación social: poblaciones expuestas al SIDA* (Madrid: Complutense, 1992). Sociological studies of Brazil have suggested an underreporting of transmission of HIV by men who have sex with men due to their unwillingness to classify themselves according to such categories as 'bisexual' or 'homosexual': see Herbert Daniel and Richard Parker, *Sexuality, Politics, and AIDS in Brazil: In Another World?* (London and Washington DC: Falmer, 1993), pp. 69–74.

15 COGAM report that the local government of Andalucía distributed thousands of faulty condoms as part of their anti-AIDS prevention and education initiatives: 'La Junta de Andalucía reconoce haber repartido miles de condones defectuosos', *Entiendes* 30 (May 1994), p. 53. An advertisement placed in the same issue of this gay magazine by the Comunidad de Madrid is clearly aimed at a male gay readership (featuring a photo of a muscular torso); yet its text gives advice to couples 'planning to have a child' (p. 52).

16 Ruth Turner and Lola Estrany, curators, *Members Only* (Barcelona: Galería Carles Poy, 12 November–20 December 1993). My thanks to David Vilaseca for providing me with a copy of the catalogue. Pepe Espaliú is represented in the exhibition.

17 For non-governmental state initiatives in Catalunya, see Antoni Mirabet i Mullol, *Funció de les organitzacions no governmentals de servei en SIDA* (Barcelona: Associació SIDA-STUDI, 1992). Other Catalan groups include: ACT-UP Barcelona; ACTUA; and Coordinadora Gai i Lesbiana, Grup Stop Sida.

18 'Inventing African AIDS', pp. 7–9; Watney, cited by Lee Edelman in 'The

Mirror and the Tank: "AIDS", Subjectivity, and the Rhetoric of Activism' in Murphy and Poirier, *Writing AIDS*, p. 13.

19 'Un día en el gueto', p. 99.

20 I take this phrase from the exhibition at the New York Public Library which coincided with massive Pride celebrations: 'Becoming Visible: The Legacy of Stonewall', 18 June to 24 September 1994. COGAM reported that in the same year Pride in Barcelona and Madrid attracted only some 750 people, a large number for Spain: *Entiendes* 30 (July 1994), p. 8.

21 Douglas Crimp and Adam Rolson, *AIDS Demo Graphics* (Seattle: Bay Press, 1990). Stephen C. Joseph ('deadlier than the virus') was New York City Commissioner of Health, appointed in 1986.

22 Another well-known national poster campaign featured the slogan 'Póntelo, pónselo' (Put [a condom] on yourself, put one on him). This campaign, much criticized by conservative moralists, is also thought to have been ineffective (*De amor y rabia*, p. 163).

23 For women and AIDS in Spain see Pilar Martínez Ten, *La mujer y el SIDA* (Madrid: Instituto de la Mujer, 1992).

24 Previously published in *Claves* 6 (October 1990).

25 Works not considered by Cortés, which establish Cardín as a major proponent of a specifically Spanish queer theory, are *Detrás por delante* (Barcelona: Laertes, 1986) and the doctoral thesis *Dialéctica y canibalismo* (Bellaterra: Universitat Autònoma de Barcelona, 1991). Cardín is also the author of a number of translations.

26 Guy Hocquenghem, *Homosexual Desire* (London: Allison & Busby, 1978), passim.

27 Alberto Cardín, *Como si nada* (Valencia: Pre-textos, 1981).

28 Eduardo Haro Ibars, *Gay Rock* (Madrid: Júcar, 1975).

29 Eduardo Haro Ibars, *Intersecciones* (Madrid: Libertarias/Prodhufi, 1991).

30 Alberto Cardín, *Despojos* (Valencia: Pre-textos, 1981).

31 Juan Vicente Aliaga, 'Speak to Me, Body: An Approach to the Work of Pepe Espaliú', in *Pepe Espaliú: 1986–93* [catalogue of the retrospective held at the Pabellón Mudéjar, Seville, May to June 1994] (Seville: Junta de Andalucía, 1994), p. 145.

32 Juan Vicente Aliaga, 'Once imágenes del tiempo: El nido', *El Europeo* (Winter 1993–94); Manel Clot, 'Once imágenes del tiempo: Carriying I [sic]', *El Europeo* (Winter 1993–94).

33 Miguel Lorenci, 'El Museo Reina Sofía rinde un homenaje póstumo a Pepe Espaliú', *Ya* (11 February 1994).

34 Adrian Searle, 'The Loss of Pepe Espaliú', in *Pepe Espaliú: Institute of Contemporary Arts, London, 4 March–17 April 1994* (London: ICA, 1994), unpaginated.

35 *Pasajes: Spanish Art Today* (Toledo: Electa, 1992), p. 74.

36 Simon Grant, 'Pepe Espaliú', *Art Monthly* (April 1994), p. 175.

37 Manel Clot, 'Dos palabras sobre el amor (Una idea del desastre)', in *Pepe Espaliú: 10 de febrero–4 de abril de 1994* (Madrid: Museo Nacional Centro de Arte Reina Sofía, 1994), unpaginated.

38 All of the works I examine below are reproduced in Aliaga's *Pepe Espaliú: 1986–93.*

39 Pepe Espaliú, *En estos cinco años* (Madrid: Estampa, 1993), p. 53 (my translation).

40 'Pepe Espaliú', *Art Monthly* (April 1994), p. 175.

41 *Ya* (11 February 1994); photo credit: EFE.

42 Haro's *Intersecciones* was, however, granted an award towards the cost of publication by the Ministry of Culture ('Dirección General del Libro y Bibliotecas'). The funding of the visual arts has recently been tilted towards private sponsorship by the so-called 'Law of Patronage'; see Rocío García, 'El mecenazgo cuenta por fin con un marco legal', *El País* (4 November 1994).

43 Gran Fury is the model of car favoured by the New York police force when working undercover.

44 In Madrid the new activism is documented every month by *Entiendes*, the journal of COGAM. Their current strategy is one of gradualist legal reform within the framework of the Spanish state constitution and the European Union; see Walter Oppenheimer, 'El Parlamento Europeo defiende la igualdad legal para los homosexuales', *El País* (9 February 1994). A more liberationist posture is taken by the smaller group La Radikal Gai. My thanks are due to Librería Berkana in Madrid, where I was able to buy most of the books I cite here.

45 Leopoldo Alas, *La acera de enfrente* (Madrid: El Papagayo, 1994), pp. 187–91. Alas is one of the very few openly gay writers to appear as such in the Spanish media.

46 I take this phrase from the title of the collection edited by Vicente Verdú, *Nuevos amores, nuevas familias* (Barcelona: Tusquets, 1992).

47 Vitoria and Valencia have pioneered same-sex domestic partnerships and adoption respectively. For studio discussion programmes with documentary segments broadcast by national television see 'Al Grano: el registro de parejas' (TVE Internacional; 9 July 1994) and 'Agora: parejas de hecho' (TVE Internacional; 28 July 94).

48 One exception to this, unmentioned by participants, is the vigorous campaign continued throughout the 1980s and 1990s by those affected by adulterated cooking oil; see Ana Llovet, '"La salud no te la devuelven": los afectados por el aceite de colza contemplan con cautela el posible cobro de las indemnizaciones', *El País* (1 September 1994). No such campaign has arisen by and for those affected by AIDS.

6

JULIO MEDEM'S *LA ARDILLA ROJA* (THE RED SQUIRREL):

A Transparent Society?

1. TRANSPARENCY, HETEROSEXUALITY, NATIONALITY

When *La ardilla roja* was released in Madrid in April 1993, reviews were unanimously hostile.[1] Echoing critical consensus in the Spanish capital, Anneli Bojstad wrote in *Screen International*:

> While it confirms the director's extraordinary visual flair, *La ardilla roja* is dogged by a weak script and unconvincing plot that fails to live up to Medem's brilliant images . . . In his ambition to embrace too many genres (love story, thriller, comedy) Medem often gets bogged down in detail. However there is enough of Medem's fresh visual style and fearless approach to confirm his growing reputation as one of Spain's most promising newcomers.[2]

Bojstad gives the key demographic of the film's target market as 'male/female 18+', significantly younger than the other Spanish release featured in the same issue, Pilar Miró's *El pájaro de la felicidad* (Bird of Happiness), classified as more appropriate for 'female[s] 25+'.

Medem, then, is thought to be a visual director par excellence; but this 'visual flair' is held to be superficial, insubstantial. Indeed one prestigious Spanish critic and author rejects *La ardilla roja* on the grounds of its supposed abuse of a single technique, one already prominent in his first, fêted feature, *Vacas* (1992): the subjective shot from the viewpoint of an animal or inanimate object: cow, squirrel, jukebox (Plate 19).[3] Peter Besas, *Variety*'s Spanish specialist, claims that in spite of the 'imaginative lensing' exemplified by such techniques 'aud[ience]s are left laughing' by the improbable plot.[4] Yet, as the subtle accounts of the film by French critics such as Philippe Rouyer suggest,[5] it is by no means clear that visual brilliance (and indeed humour) preclude serious concerns. Indeed Medem, a commentator on his own work as articulate as Almodóvar, albeit less flamboyant in persona, has himself suggested a framework within which word and image (meaning and sensation) can be reconciled.

The pressbook to *La ardilla roja* contains an unusually literate essay by the director which begins by stressing the ethical and political dimensions of the plot, which are linked to the cinematic resource of perspective: '[*La ardilla roja*] is an anti-macho parable in the form of a mystery comedy. A fictional story seen from the point of view of the male psyche from which we learn a moral lesson about the feeling of ownership men impose upon women.'[6] But that 'moral lesson' is no simple didacticism, for, as Medem notes and as we shall see, the protagonists' 'love is born from a lie' and takes place in a context of parody and performance: the eponymous Red Squirrel camping site in La Rioja in which the main couple and secondary characters alike play out their amatory and familial roles. For Medem the 'mystery' of the Emma Suárez character (an amnesiac known variously as Lisa and Sofía) precipitates the 'game' which articulates the narrative. The game is founded on the unknowability of a woman whose identity has been 'invented' by her new-found male lover Jota (Nancho Novo) and who can but glimpse 'the darker and [more] turbulent side of the story' beneath the 'visible' evidence of the 'deception' which Jota has himself produced: 'a beautiful woman tailor-made for him' (pressbook).

In this chapter I will suggest that this depth metaphor which unites woman and landscape (feminine 'mystery' beneath the skin, natural enigmas beneath the surface of the reservoir by which the action takes place) is called into question by the action of the film itself. Stubbornly invisible, in spite of all the efforts of Medem's conspicuous technical flair, female sexuality and national identity are not so much hidden as called into being by the ardent attention of the lover, just as in the intricate narrative of *La ardilla roja* true love follows from a lie. But I will also suggest that in the baroque ostentation of his visual language and in his concern for technology, truth, violence and play, Medem coincides with the most influential theorist of postmodernism in Spain, Italian nihilist philosopher Gianni Vattimo.[7]

For some twenty years Vattimo has proposed a 'weakened' form of epistemology and ontology, in the wake of Nietzsche and Heidegger, which would not be simply an apology for the society of the spectacle and which would still enable us to articulate the quest for such latterly unfashionable concepts as 'freedom' and 'happiness'. And recently he has reworked this continuing problematic around a broadly visual theme, that of 'transparency'.[8] What is the 'transparent society' for Vattimo? It is the society of unlimited communication in which the mass media tend towards absolute spirit: 'the perfect selfconsciousness by everyone of everything that happens in real time'.[9] However, the ideal of transparency held out by the endless expansion of the 'logic of information', the ideal which posits a definitive and normative order in which 'the map is wholly identified with the territory' (p. 81) has contradictory effects. When 'everything is converted into an object of communication' Vattimo does not find the totalizing homologation of, say, Virilio but rather 'an explosion of visions of the world' (p. 79), not self-consciousness without remainder but 'oscillation, plurality, and erosion of the reality principle' (p. 82). It is in this chaos, opacity and *extraña-miento* (alienation, banishment, nostalgia) that Vattimo finds hope, however tenuous, for liberation 'through the local . . . the dialect[al], through particularity and contingency' (p. 84).

We will return to the implications of this theory in the second half of this chapter when I compare Medem's 'weak' version of Basque identity to that of another apostate of nationalism, Fernando Savater. More immediately relevant here is Vattimo's identification of the false transparency of contemporary society with the visual apparatus of cinema. Vattimo juxtaposes Benjamin's 'shock' of technology ('the constant stream of projectiles to which the viewer must readapt') with Heidegger's *Stoss* (also 'shock': 'the thrownness into the world', the anguish of mortality and uprootedness).[10] Like Benjamin's emblematic pedestrian picking a way through city traffic, the cinema spectator is caught in a 'rapid succession of images . . . demanding a labour of recomposition and readaptation' (p. 142). It is a situation of 'homelessness' which (as in Heidegger) is not provisional, but constitutive (p. 143). Citing Heidegger's difficult concept of 'earth' (as 'other, nothing, universal gratuitousness, and insignificance'),[11] Vattimo claims that the role of aesthetic experience is now precisely that of 'keeping uprootedness alive' (p. 142): 'Against the nostalgia for eternity (of the work) and nostalgia for authenticity (of experience) we must recognise that the shock is all that remains of the creativity of art in the age of generalized communication' (p. 151). Citing cinematic perception as a model for the 'excitability and hypersensitivity' of urban man, whose experience is one of 'minimal and continual variations' (p. 151), Vattimo reveals a characteristically friendly attitude towards technological innovation. Thus he claims that the 'superficiality and precariousness of the aesthetic experience of late modernity are not necessarily signs of alienation [but rather] a weakening of the reality principle' (p. 153); or again, the society of spectacle may lead to the manipulation of images by power, but it is also 'a society in which reality takes on a weak and more fluid nature, a society in which experience acquires the character of oscillation, deracination, and play' (p. 154). When we understand that 'ambiguity is not provisional [but] constitutive of art', then we may hope that 'art can present itself (not yet, but ultimately) as creativity and freedom'.

Let us see how Vattimo's aesthetics of oscillation are played out in the bravura opening sequence of *La ardilla roja*. The opening credits play over an eerie underwater sequence showing what we later learn to be a submerged forest that has been flooded to make the reservoir where the protagonists go camping. The film proper begins with Jota (saturnine Nancho Novo) contemplating suicide by a broiling sea in San Sebastián. Shot in showy high and low angles in which he appears, alternately, to be suspended helplessly over the waves and to loom massively over the beach, Jota's as yet motiveless despair (he has been ditched by his girlfriend) is heightened by unexplained cutaways to a window overlooking the beach (his own apartment?) and to a motorbike approaching at speed. Plunging over the parapet on to the beach, the as yet unidentified motorcyclist is literally thrown to earth, the pitted sand resembling the lunar surface, a visual association heightened by her astronautlike helmet. The first dialogue exchange between the two main characters (Jota has followed her down to the beach) is shot, ostentatiously once more, with each face shown subjectively (from the other partner's viewpoint) upside down. Interrogating the newcomer ('Hey, you're a girl'), Jota not only discovers her amnesia, he also, immediately, takes advantage of it to lie. As the camera gives an extreme close-up of Suárez's brown eyes we hear Jota tell her character that those same eyes are blue: 'blue, tangled eyes'. It is an exploitation of editing overlap (a refusal to cut 'straight across' sound and vision tracks[12]) which will prove typical of the film.

Formally and thematically, the sequence is paradigmatic of Vattimo's 'art of oscillation'. Lisa's fall is quite literally a shock, a projection or throwing into the world to which the spectator (in the narrative, in the cinema) must immediately readapt. Moreover that world is a tabula rasa; or more properly a land or earth (the beach) whose traces do not signify and which reveal no sign of habitation. Established immediately as an amnesiac, Lisa's rootlessness is constitutive, not provisional, and Medem's aesthetic project will aim throughout the film to keep that sense of exile or banishment alive. Moreover the nature of this twin encounter (between the characters, between the spectator and the film) is hermeneutic, in the broadest sense. As Vattimo puts it: 'the encounter with the work of art . . . is like an encounter with a person who has a vision of the world with which ours has to be confronted in an interpretative fashion' (p. 141). Vattimo gives this aesthetic dialogue the Heideggerian tag 'the putting into work of truth'. But it is typical of Medem that this work should be founded on a lie: the substitution of blue eyes for brown, the first strand in the tangled web of the plot.

Benjamin's pedestrian found the 'danger of the loss of life' a precondition of modern urbanism; Medem's motorcyclist is also marked primordially by mortality. But the seriousness of such concerns is not necessarily diluted by the excitability and hypersensitivity of La ardilla roja's visual technique. Rather, as the film develops, we see that such an intensification of aesthetic experience is characteristic of the society of generalized communication, whose supposed transparency is dangerously and fruitfully muddied by the possibilities of performance and play afforded by the mass media. Thus when 'Lisa' is taken to the hospital Jota improvises her name and past as his supposed girlfriend. But the male hospital orderly to whom he gives this invented biography is engaged in yet more elaborate role play: calling a radio phone-in and impersonating a lonely housewife in an oblique (and later successful) attempt to seduce the young petrol attendant who works in the garage opposite his window. Mass media promise immediacy, total awareness of the world and presence to self. Instead they deliver a chance for opacity and chaos. The song requested by the orderly in the hospital (Nat King Cole's 'Let There Be Love') is also heard on the car radio of Lisa's psychotic husband. And significantly, the orderly (who will prove to be Lisa's brother) is not embarrassed when Jota witnesses his deception. In homo, as in heterosexual, pursuit, the lover may oscillate between self-identification and *extrañamiento* or wilful alienation. The film thus places no particular emphasis on the sexual preference of its characters (later the camp site will be graced by a couple of lesbian waitresses): as in Vattimo's nihilist ontology, identity 'does not necessarily coincide with the stable, fixed, and permanent, but rather with event, consensus, dialogue, and interpretation' (p. 87).

Jota effectively kidnaps Lisa from the city hospital and has her drive the motorcycle to the rural camping site. But this return to nature (burlesqued in the Basque site's implausible claim to possess a 'Mediterranean atmosphere') is framed by visual and auditory technologies: as Jota packs, the unwatched television shows an earnest documentary on the shy but combative red squirrel; Lisa is shown still photographs in the hospital which (subjectively) start into motion; the camping site jukebox which looks out at Lisa plays the same song by Jota's former band that we have heard in a dream or fantasy sequence as the couple are riding down the highway. In a further, violent example of contamination and simultaneity, the downtrodden housewife whom Lisa befriends at the campsite (Carmen: María Barranco) washes the dishes to the radio as, in an unestablished location elsewhere, Lisa's unseen husband Félix (Carmelo Gómez) runs down a hapless pedestrian to the sound of the same song ('Let There Be Love' once more). Thus, as the ideal of social transparency becomes ever more technically possible (as the characters are granted mediatized connections with one another), so that ideal becomes ever more unthinkable (none of the characters can be sure what those connections signify). And if, as Vattimo claims, transparency 'functions only from the point of view of a central subject' (p. 105), then that subject (Jota, who has imposed his name and past on the woman) comes under increasing pressure in the second act of the film: Jota cannot see the invisible squirrel accessible to the privileged gaze of Lisa and a young girl at the camping site; and when he is knocked unconscious by a pine cone strategically dropped by the squirrel Lisa parrots back to him the words with which he initially interrogated her ('What colour are your eyes?').

And if the machista rolls from the centre, then his discourse proves stubbornly untransparent, disturbingly opaque. We have seen that social communication is not instrumental but substantial (the connections between the characters are achieved through technological mediation); but *La ardilla roja* questions the possibility of an ideal communicative community in which (to cite Vattimo) 'the demand for truth in language requires the elimination of any obstacle to the transparency of communication; especially of objects deliberately placed by subjects' (p. 99). It does this by making truth dependent on fable or lie. Thus, as Medem notes in the pressbook, 'all the feelings that grow are born from Jota's original lie, giving them a true psychological motive. They are born at a moment in which Jota has already died a little on the rocks and when Lisa has forgotten everything about her past.' This is not only (as Medem claims) a parody of male chauvinism; it is also a challenge to the metaphysical notion of truth as a simple equation between a proposition and a state of affairs in the world. Within each little narrative (each spiralling lie on the part of both Jota and Lisa) the characters experience their improvised roles as authentic. Indeed, as Philippe Rouyer notes, in a kind of parody of the linguistic performative, it suffices for a character to pronounce something in order for it to come true: Lisa claims, implausibly, to be a champion swimmer, but then shows evidence of uncanny skill when racing a youth in the reservoir; or again, the couple's graphic retelling of the (invented) memories of sexual acts they claim to have shared ('I love it when you bite me all over') precedes and intensifies the pleasure they experience in the act itself, when finally they make love for the first time.

But this structural primacy of fabulation also relates to nature and myth. The faith in self-transparency requires nature to serve as an object to be dominated (Vattimo, p. 106). Nature in *La ardilla roja*, however, is opaque and inscrutable, gifted with its own impossible perspective (the scurrying, inverted point of view of the squirrel descending the tree). The giant painted cutout of a squirrel that stands at the entrance to the camp site is a parodic pointer to the degradation and the persistence of an animistic spirit of the place. In this fabulation of the world, then, we find a certain return to or of myth, but in an ironic or 'weakened' way which avoids Vattimo's three pitfalls of archaism, cultural relativism and 'moderate irrationalism' (p. 115). Thus Medem's appeal to the forest and lake as sites of feminine or ethnic mystery does not imply a return to an 'authentic relation of man to self and nature' or an 'attack on scientific-technical civilization'; and it does not suggest that a 'study of other civilisations' (such as the rustic) 'might help us understand our own' urban anomie. Nor, finally, does it imply that certain fields of knowledge (femininity, nationality, affectivity) are immune to rationality while others are not. Rather it demonstrates the 'secularism' of Vattimo in which 'a secularized culture is not simply a culture that has turned its back on the religious contents of tradition, but one which continues living them as traces, or as models that are covered and distorted, but profoundly present' (p. 129). I will suggest later that such is the status of a resonant absence in *La ardilla roja*: Basque nationalism. It is enough here to note the persistent and puzzling *frayage* of the trace in its irreducible materiality: the tracks of the squirrel under the tree (which Jota mistakes, or claims to mistake, for those of a rat), the food and faeces which it lets fall on oblivious males. The humorous tone of such moments ensures that they are read as ironic, even as they take on affective weight in the narrative: 'myth recovers legitimacy, but only within the framework of a general experience of "weakened" truth' (Vattimo, p. 131). Like Jota's unlikely pop group, shown in druidlike costumes battering prehistoric instruments, such mythical moments are 'not the contrary, but the consequence of modernization', of the progressive taking leave of a technocratic rationalism which has reached its end. Just as truth cannot be distinguished from lie in the fabulation of authentic emotion, so myth cannot fully be corralled off, uncontaminated by the modern and the rational: as the group pound their instruments a jet flies low overhead.

To say that truth is not simply what it was before is not to say there can be no ethical or political discrimination. And the last act of the film raises with typical visual flair the problem of violence and identification. If Jota and Lisa's self-invented love affair corresponds to Vattimo's heterotopia of 'lightened being' (of 'what is dispersed and affirmed in the difference of not being presence, stability, structure'),[13] then the ironically named Félix, Lisa's brutal husband, represents strong being with a vengeance: tracking down the lovers to the camp site and challenged to demonstrate the visceral love for Lisa which he claims, Félix cuts off his own cheek and challenges Jota for possession of Lisa (Plate 20). Yet, as we shall see, heterosexuality cannot be reduced to domination in *La ardilla roja*; and national identity is also not to be derived from confrontation or competition in a 'strong' sense.

2. HOW THE REAL WORLD BECAME A FICTION

Alberto Iglesias's fine score for *La ardilla roja* cites *Vertigo*: a swelling, spiralling motif which underlines the male subject's entanglement with a female object which his own desire has put into play. However, unlike Hitchcock's Scotty (James Stewart), Medem's Jota does not seek, violently, to elucidate the feminine enigma and to draw her into the light which is fatal to her. This is because, as we have seen, the psychological truth of the characters is shown (to us, to them) to be founded on falsehood. Indeed, the lies improvised by Jota as the narrative progresses prove literally to be true: thus Lisa is indeed being pursued by an insane husband, as the inventive Jota tells the inquisitive family with whom they share the camp site. A related theme here is sleep or dream (*sueño*). If, in Vattimo's Nietzschean tag, 'the real world has become a fiction', then we must, in a further Nietzschean paradox, 'continue dreaming knowing that one is dreaming' (p. 84). It is a formula which describes both the playful irony of the characters improvising true, heterosexual love, and the ambiguous tone of Medem's text, oscillating between rhapsodic lyricism à la *Vertigo* and critical disengagement. At one point Lisa whispers: 'My eyes are tangled in sleep.'

As we shall see, it is in a late dream sequence that truth and gender are most fatally entangled. But let us first examine Medem's reproduction of feminine stereotypes in a radically weakened form. Lisa is visually identified with the squirrel: dressed in red and brown, falling to earth at one point from high in a tree. And as the embodiment of a mysterious 'nature' she is also pure physiology: we are given repeated extreme close-ups of the downy hair on her arms rising in goose flesh, in an apparent intuition of the approach of her husband. In a disturbing sequence, she invites a young boy to put his hand down her jeans and 'bites' it with her vagina (there is a very brief extreme close-up here). Lisa is accused of insanity by her husband, but her mental state is never definitively confirmed to the viewer.

Yet these stereotypes (of physiology, castration and hysteria) are suspended or evacuated by both the relations depicted between women and men in the film and the nature of Emma Suárez's performance and persona. Thus gender identity is shown to be relational and contingent: in the very first scene on the beach Lisa reverses Jota's question to her by asking him: 'Who are *you*?' And if the squirrel is the female principle, then its invisibility is shared for most of *La ardilla roja* by the film's most brutally masculine character: Lisa's husband Félix, who remains unseen until the third act. One typically visual, wordless sequence shows the reversibility of gender roles: as Lisa steers the motorbike Jota, seated behind her, secretly caresses her hair with his fingers, believing her to be unaware of his attention. Then he catches sight of Lisa's ironic look in the mirror and sees his own look caught by her gaze.

Such sequences are always qualified and complexified by Suárez's intelligent performance, which mixes frank sensuality with ironic sensibility. Moon-faced, fair and innocent, still she can seem knowing and self-assured. Medem himself cites the way in which she combines the qualities of a 'naive little girl' and a 'sexually sophisticated [*viciosa*] woman',[14] a persona reinforced by her screen history. Suárez's career began at age fourteen when she played an 'innocent child' in a TV series,[15] and now nearing thirty she can barely shake the 'Lolita' tag.[16] Insisting throughout her career that she 'did not wish to be treated as a sex object',[17] but taking high-profile, sexually graphic roles (such as the incestuous sister of Antonio Banderas),[18] Suárez could hardly avoid that trial of visibility to which female stars are subjected. When she posed on the cover of a listings supplement for her next film, with tousled hair, bare midriff and silver miniskirt, Suárez was given the caption 'Who will bell this cat?'[19] Beyond infantilism and animal physicality, however, Suárez's persona embodies a certain challenge to and independence of the male spectator, a challenge that is memorably exploited by Medem. If she is indeed a cat or squirrel she is clearly one that bites.

Such discontinuities and contradictions suggest that in *La ardilla roja* heterosexuality traces a hermeneutic logic in which gender roles are to be read not as conformity to a state of being outside the film but rather as correspondence or dialogue within the multiple fabulations of which the film is composed. Thus the squirrel is the shy and mysterious feminine principle (Lisa); but it is also the combative male partner, who may lose its tail fighting over a mate (Félix). Moreover, as Philippe Rouyer notes (p. 53),

Jota is also explicitly identified with the squirrel: both have lightning reflexes (the young man can catch a falling glass; the animal spirits away a fallen prawn). Moreover, Jota's seduction of Lisa requires him, repeatedly, to adopt a position gendered as feminine. When slapped by a macho fellow camper for 'failing to keep his girlfriend in line' he replies simply: 'I have no balls.' Lisa claims (playfully, dismissively, lovingly?) that Jota can do nothing but 'cook, fuck and lie' (the domestic, sexual and discursive roles traditionally assigned to women). In the extended and dramatic dream sequence in which Félix is first shown to the spectator, he repeats to Jota the words Jota had first said to Lisa on the beach ('Hey, you're a girl') before beating his unresponsive male rival to a pulp. Such sequences at once preserve, empty and distort traditional stereotypes: Jota may claim to be a 'girl', but the dream still relies on the standard male rivalry structure of the homo-social triangle; and he may be best at cooking and fucking, but still he can erect the motorcycle vertical in the sandy ground of the camp site, a phallic spectacle which merits Lisa's erotic admiration (or so she claims).

Medem, then, does not simply subscribe to a rejection of gender stereotype and an indifferent sexual relativism. Rather, in Vattimo's words, his 'liquidation of the myth of transparency' (in this case, of masculine or feminine presence to self) tends towards 'a less ideological attitude towards experience of the world, which rather than the object of "objective" knowledge, is the place of the production of symbolic systems . . . which are historical, that is narratives situated at a critical distance . . . which know and offer themselves as "transformation", never claiming to be "nature"' (p. 109). Rendered opaque and historicized, held at a critical and ironic distance, still gender roles persist and are lived 'weakly' in the bodies of Medem's protagonists.

A further and yet more mysterious trace is left in La ardilla roja by Basque nationalism. Medem himself has claimed that the film 'could be set anywhere'; and that, although based himself in San Sebastián, he finds the 'overblown' nationalist atmosphere 'asphyxiating'.[20] It is perhaps significant that the features of a director invariably described as 'Basque' by the Madrid media are funded by the central government, not the Basque autonomous area which has, nonetheless, been active in its sponsorship of other local directors.[21] The attitude implied by La ardilla roja is reminiscent of another reluctant but affectionate resident of San

Sebastián, philosopher Fernando Savater. An avowed anarchist and apostate, Savater has consistently written 'against fatherlands' at considerable personal risk from those who support the 'strongest' models of nationhood.[22] Savater proposes (like the nihilist Vattimo) a radical scepticism towards identity which, he believes, leads in the case of regionalism to the mere reproduction of state totalization (p. 12): self-identification, even on the part of minorities, is achieved through exclusion and confrontation (p. 26), based on cheap folklore and mystificatory biologism (p. 35) and rationalized retrospectively by appeal to a fetishized past (p. 67). Savater proposes, in typically fragmented and dispersed texts, a new understanding of nationalism as 'performative' (p. 19) in which (as in Vattimo once more) being is radically weakened and no longer understood as violent confrontation (p. 112). 'Demilitarizing' Basque nationalism would not, however, be to render it transparent or unproblematic: rather it would be to stress conflict (*pólemos*) in a Heideggerian sense: as (non-totalizing) difference, as unfolding (ex-plication) and as mutual recognition of self in the other (p. 114). 'Denying the fatherland [*patria*]', concludes Savater, 'is to return to individuals the ability to invent and to forget, to be different and to be new, to be free and to think for themselves' (p. 207).

This would seem to be a fine anticipation of *La ardilla roja*'s plot, based as the latter is on the opportunities afforded by invention and amnesia, the forging of new and different roles, and the chance of freedom which lies in the loss of a transparent (unexamined) relation to the land and to myth. But, with the theme of Basque identity wholly invisible in *La ardilla roja*, how can it be called a Basque film? The camp site is said to be in La Rioja, a liminal area split between Basque Alava (Araba) and Castile. However, much of the film was shot on location in Madrid's scrubby Casa de Campo. Moreover, despite the unequivocally Basque names of many of the cast and crew, the principal roles go to outsiders: Suárez is from Madrid, Nancho Novo a veteran of the Galician music scene (a past with which the script assumes its youthful audience to be familiar), María Barranco remains best known as the Andalusian model Candela in Almodóvar's *Mujeres al borde de un ataque de nervios* (Women on the Verge of a Nervous Breakdown, 1988).

For Vattimo, we remember, a communicative community is a normative ideal, one based on totalizing self-transparency and the 'liquidation of obstacles and opacities' (p. 101). For Medem, Basques, barely seen or heard as such in the film, would appear to be the opposite of Vattimo's dominant, central subjects: 'subject-objects of reflexive knowledge'. Yet still their trace persists in weakened and distorted form. I have already mentioned the forest and lake, mythic sites of a famously rural people; and the shy squirrel, the image of a stereotypically taciturn and unforthcoming race.[23] Like homosexuality, which is noted but not underlined in *La ardilla roja*, the Basqueness of personal names, of physical types, of topography and toponymics (for example, Donosti for San Sebastián) goes unremarked within the diegesis. But it is precisely this taken-for-grantedness which confirms the allusion to a lived community which need no longer present itself as either mythical or military, whose identity is predicated neither on the past nor on a confrontation with the other, a confrontation which could only mutely replicate the totalizing terror to which Basques have historically been subjected. Hence Medem with the lightest of touches (a face, a voice, a name) gestures towards what Vattimo calls a critical 'liberation through the local' which can occur only outside of terror: 'only when dialects acquire visibility do they discern their own grammar' and hence gain access to a 'sceptical awareness of the historicity and contingency of all dialects' (p. 84).[24]

Vattimo is at pains to distinguish this localism or dialectalism from the 'brute manifestation of immediacy'. But we might read the brutally immediate terroristic violence of Lisa's husband as a displacement of the historically and politically specific violence of ETA which Medem does not care to represent directly. Once more traditions, of whatever kind, are not simply erased; rather they persist in distorted or degraded form: Félix's hit-and-run victims and his self-severed cheek reveal that, in spite of the ludic and oneiric tone of much of the film, terror is still lived as a trace in Basque bodies, albeit a trace that is subject to an ironic and sceptical reinterpretation. This 'weakening' (evacuation, distortion but not abandonment) of nationalism is not, of course, unique to Medem. Even a film such as Imanol Uribe's fast-paced thriller *Días contados* (Running Out of Time, 1994), which is explicitly set in a terrorist milieu, disavows a political violence which is no longer held to be central, focusing rather on the psychological dimensions of a romance between an ETA commando and his youthful junkie lover.[25]

One further example of the persistence of tradition and its relation to nationality is film form itself. In spite of its self-conscious modernity and virtuoso visual effects, *La ardilla roja* preserves many aspects of that classical model known as 'Hollywood'. Thus the plot corresponds to pragmatic, neo-Aristotelian models currently promoted by screenwriters in the United States.[26] Medem follows the three-act structure of 'establish, build, and resolve': the opening amnesia and lie (Act I) lead to increasing entanglements (Act II) which are themselves violently curbed by the intervention of Lisa's husband (Act III). Medem also ensures audience identification with his central character in traditional style by using such devices as introducing him immediately, placing him in jeopardy and making his eyes those of the audience (p. 72). And he maximizes emotion through such carefully controlled structural techniques as pace, graduation and foreshadowing (p. 108). The preservation of these forms makes the film attractive to the young, Americanized audience, the 'key demographic' which *Film International* predicted for it.[27] Yet like gender stereotypes and references to Basque identification, these classical structures are emptied and distorted even as they are preserved. For the undecidability of Medem's fable (the dependence of truth on lie) means that the audience cannot hold tight to a crucial distinction common in current Hollywood products: that between outer and inner motivation, described by one pedagogue as, respectively, 'what the character visibly hopes to accomplish by the end of the movie' and 'the reason for the outer motivation which the character thinks will lead to self-worth' (Hauge, p. 72). While Jota's outer motivation is clear enough (he aims to seduce Lisa by imposing his narrative on her), his inner motivation remains opaque, since he and we remain uncertain as to the veracity of Lisa's amnesia and the authenticity of her love. *La ardilla roja* thus splits along the line of the visible: between exterior and interior, message and theme, conscious and unconscious.[28]

Medem has presented himself in the press as part of a new generation of Spanish directors, characterized by their attention to cutting and camera style.[29] As I have suggested, however, this stress on the visual does not preclude a continuing meditation on sombre themes held to be characteristic of an earlier, more sober Spanish cinema. Indeed, like Heidegger's conception of the work of art, *La ardilla roja* is indelibly marked by mortality and earth: rescued from the car which Félix has plunged into the reservoir in pursuit of Lisa, Jota intones on the radio: 'I have seen death very close. At the bottom of the lake it smelled of earth.' Like Vattimo's heterotopia, *La ardilla roja* is at once a symptom of 'the ornamental . . . explosion of the aesthetic today' and, beyond its flashy visuals, a pointer which 'connects the transformed aesthetic experience of mass society with the Heideggerian call for an experience of being that is not (or no longer) metaphysical' (p. 172). If Medem's third feature has as its working title *Tierra* (Earth), then it is most unlikely that that term is to be taken in any foundational sense. The fresh and intelligent humour of *La ardilla roja*, which Vattimo might identify, problematically, with the 'Latin accent' and 'the lighter social rationality' he perceives in the Spanish state (p. 70), is critical as well as simply pleasurable. *La ardilla roja* is thus one answer to the question posed to Spain by Vattimo and to Vattimo by Spain:

> Is it possible to perform [*actuar*] an emancipation which opens existence up to its potential for immediate pleasure, that is, which brings us closer to happiness . . . without having to pass through the violence which revolution entails and exerts in revolutionary militants? The hope of a revolution which would be performed through a *small* distortion in the meaning of the mediatizations of our life attempts to find and to give a positive response to this question. (p. 71)

It is a question of crucial relevance to the autonomous region of the Basque Country/Euskadi and the Spanish state to which it still belongs. But that lightness of being, that small, aesthetic distortion, does not preclude interiority: in the final sequence of *La ardilla roja* Jota tracks the missing Lisa/Sofía down to the squirrel enclosure at the Madrid zoo and tells her, 'You still don't know what I have inside me.' As she looks on, smiling, he is rewarded by falling faeces courtesy of the ever-invisible rodent. But the answer to the enigma of male interiority is given in the song which plays over the credits and whose lyrics are by Medem himself: inside the male lover lies 'a lighter, more verdant [*frondosa*] life'. In a society of generalized communication, a society which violently seeks to impose the transparency of totalizing self-consciousness, a lightness of life is no negligible ambition. It is one realized by the small, 'weak' distortions of Medem's extraordinary visual flair.

NOTES

1 One exception was trade journal *Cineinforme* which praised the 'impact' of the film's images and the 'innovatory vision' of its camerawork; *Cineinforme* 639–40 (July 1993), p. 51. The director of photography is Gonzalo F. Berridi.

2 Anneli Bojstad's review in *Screen International* 905 (30 April 1993), p. 16.

3 Augusto M. Torres, *Diccionario del cine español* (Madrid: Espasa Calpe, 1994), p. 471. *Vacas* won the Gold Prize in the Young Cinema section of the Tokyo Film Festival of 1992 and the BFI Sutherland Award for first feature. Spanish and Catalan critics frequently stressed both the 'look of the cow' and the 'situations of great visual force' in *Vacas*; I take these phrases from Angel Quintana's review, 'Violència y bogeria vistes per unes vaques', *Punt* [Gerona] (30 May 1992). Quintana also claims that while the film is 'profoundly Basque' its position with respect to such historical questions as the Civil War is unclear, with Medem and his characters choosing simply to observe, without becoming involved.

4 Peter Besas's review in *Variety* (10 May 1993), p. 238.

5 Philippe Rouyer, '*L'Ecureuil rouge*: double jeu', *Positif* 398 (April 1994), pp. 52–3.

6 Pressbook (London: Metro Tartan, 30 September 1994). Metro Tartan are also the film's UK video distributors; neither *Vacas* nor *La ardilla roja* has received a US theatrical release, although it was reported that a Hollywood remake of the latter was planned; see Tom Charity, 'Basque in Glory', *Time Out* [London] (28 September–5 October 1994), p. 18. As the following synopsis shows, the US romantic comedy *While You Were Sleeping* (Jon Turteltaub, 1995) repeats *La ardilla roja*'s plot while reversing its gender roles: '[Peter] Gallagher falls for [Sandra] Bullock, literally. Right after they meet, he tumbles onto some train tracks and ends up comatose. Bullock goes with him to the hospital and when his family arrives, they think she's his fiancée.'; anon., *Premiere* [New York] (May 1995), p. 21.

7 For an introduction to Vattimo's work, see my 'Gianni Vattimo: Philosopher of Post-modernity', *Revista de estudios hispánicos* 25 (1991), pp. 109–16. Vattimo remains best known for *La fine della modernità* (Milan: Garzanti, 1985). The term most associated with him is the coinage 'weak thought'.

8 Gianni Vattimo, *La sociedad transparente*, trans. Teresa Oñate (Barcelona: Paidós, 1990); Italian original, published 1989. The Spanish translation contains a specially written preface by the author.

9 *La sociedad transparente*, p. 80. All translations from Vattimo are my own.

10 *La sociedad transparente*, pp. 139, 140.

11 *La sociedad transparente*, p. 144.

12 I am not suggesting this is in itself an avant-garde editing technique. Hollywood veteran Edward Dmytryk recommends 'keep[ing] it fresh

and fast with the overlap' especially in dialogue exchanges: 'A cutter who cuts "straight across" because overlapping takes more time and greater effort . . . puts out a film which falls short of its potential'; Edward Dmytryk, *On Film Editing* (Boston and London: Focal, 1984), p. 35.

13 *La sociedad transparente*, p. 172.

14 Beatrice Sartori, ' "Me interesa mucho seducir", dice Julio Medem: director revelación con *Vacas* ultima el rodaje de su segunda película, *La ardilla roja*', *El Mundo* (4 October 1992). In this interview Medem confirms once more the visual origin of his cinema, whose source, he claims, is never discursive.

15 Isabel de Villaleriga, 'Emma Suárez', *La Vanguardia* [magazine] (November 1988). The series was an adaptation of Rosa Chacel's *Memorias de Leticia Valle*.

16 Carlos Ferrando, 'Emma Suárez, una niña bien para José Coronado', *Diario 16* (27 August 1990). Suárez herself notes the contradiction between her 'sweet face' and the 'complex characters' she is asked to play; Diego Muñoz, 'Emma Suárez: el éxito de una actriz "maldita"', *El País* (25 September 1990).

17 Anon., 'Emma Suárez: "No quiero ser objeto de deseo" ', *Diez Minutos* (12 April 1988). Suárez is photographed in this feature with her strap falling seductively off her shoulder.

18 In Paco Periñán's *Contra el viento* (Against the Wind,1990).

19 'Emma Suárez: ¿quién le pone el cascabel a esta gata?', *El País de las Tentaciones* [Friday Supplement] (14 October 1994). The piece inside, by Alfonso Rivera, was to promote her then current role as the lover of foot fetishist Miguel Bosé in José Miguel Ganga's lurid *Enciende mi pasión* (Light My Fire).

20 Diego Muñoz, 'Julio Medem pasa del campo al cámping: el director de *Vacas* rueda *La ardilla roja*', *El País* (5 October 1992).

21 In the interview with Muñoz, Medem states that of the 170 million peseta budget 65 million came from the Ministry of Culture in Madrid. *La ardilla roja*'s TV rights were later sold, with those of *Kika*, to Canal + whose parent company is French; anon., 'Canal + adquiere los derechos de emisión de la práctica totalidad del cine español', *El País* (31 August 1994). Canal + went on to part fund Medem's third feature, *Tierra*. Subsidized Basque filmmakers active in the 1980s and 1990s include Pedro Olea, Imanol Uribe (born in El Salvador) and Montxo Armendáriz. See the unpublished paper by Xon de Ros, '*Vacas* and Basque Cinema: The Making of a Tradition'. John Hopewell's indispensable *El cine español después de Franco* (Madrid: Arquero, 1989) gives a survey of Basque cinema in the transition to democracy (pp. 313–23). The principal historian of Basque film is Santos Zunzunegui.

22 I cite from Fernando Savater, *Contra las patrias* (Barcelona: Tusquets, 1984). The prolific Savater is also known as a film critic and novelist.

23 One history of Basque literature derives the lack of lyric poetry in the language from the supposedly 'reserved and taciturn character of

Basque speakers' and their 'flight from intimate confessions'; L. M. Mujika, *Historia de la literatura euskerika* (San Sebastián: Haranburu, 1979), p. 12.

24 Critics had already noted the ambivalent status of the Basque Country/Euskadi in Medem's earlier *Vacas*: F. Marinero wrote in *El Mundo* (6–12 March 1992) that 'the Basque Country is half analysed , half sublimated'; Nuria Vidal wrote in *Fotogramas* (May 1992) that *Vacas* showed 'sixty years of history [but was] not historical'. Philippe Rouyer calls the video clip in *La ardilla roja* an 'astute retrieval [*récupération*] of Basque culture' (p. 53).

25 For an account of a more explicit, but equally problematic, Basque director of the 1970s, see my 'Eloy de la Iglesia's Cinema of Transition', in *Laws of Desire: Questions of Homosexuality in Spanish Writing and Film 1960–1990* (Oxford: Oxford University Press, 1992), pp. 129–62. A certain tension between the demands of nationalism and the lure of foreign glamour can be seen in the earliest, silent Basque cinema. A lobby card for Mauro Azkona's *El mayorazgo de Basterretxe* (The Heir of Basterretxe, 1928) both proudly announces 'a national film in a Basque setting' and defensively warns: 'This is not a superproduction, nor a cinematic masterpiece. It is simply a national picture which you will enjoy watching.' Reproduced in Alberto López Echevarrieta, *Cine vasco: ¿realidad o ficción?* (Bilbao: Mensajero, no date), opposite p. 129. My thanks to Leah Middlebrook for providing me with a copy of this book.

26 Michael Hauge, *Writing Screenplays That Sell* (New York: Harper, 1991). For an earlier account, more directed towards adaptations, see Edward Dmytryk, *On Screen Writing* (Boston and London: Focal, 1985).

27 In the interview by Tom Charity in *Time Out* cited above, Medem also drew attention to the film's greater success in Barcelona than in Madrid.

28 For Hauge the 'inner' motivation of the hero is related to the 'theme' of the movie which (unlike its overt message) may be unconscious to both character and screenwriter.

29 John Hopewell, 'Spotlight: Cannes Preview: Spain', *Variety* (15–21 May 1995), pp. C15, C38. This piece was written as Medem wrapped his third feature, *Tierra* (Earth); it begins, however, with a reference to the notorious squirrel point of view in *La ardilla roja*.

CONCLUSION:

Images That Speak in Silence

The first historian of Spanish film in the 1990s speaks of a 'farewell to optimism'.[1] The phrase is poorly chosen: the industry had survived in a state of perpetual crisis since it began. But John Hopewell noted that the new globalization and homogenization of the media industries posed a threat to the local and regional particularity of Spanish cinema, even though much of that cinema was (as he remarks with characteristic acerbity) 'vulgar, dull, and ineffectual'.[2]

The subsidized quality cinema of the 1980s had proved to be a commercial dead end: *Bernarda Alba* rated no higher than number thirty-two on the list of grosses for domestic features from the years 1986–89.[3] Yet at the San Sebastián festival of 1993 not all was gloomy. Trade journal *Moving Pictures* reported in its 'complete breakdown of the Spanish audiovisual industry' ('Homage to Iberia') that the decline of state subsidy had led producers energetically to seek alternative financing sources in vertical integration, world sales, the new private television networks and even Latin America.[4] It was symptomatic of new and more flexible arrangements that the Basque film financing board, Euskal Media, made no demands that projects be shot in Basque or in the País Vasco/Euskadi; and local company Igeldo Zine Produkzioak was reported to have collaborated with Mexican production houses on 'an ironic musical about the US invasion of Panama' (Paul Leduc's *Dollar Mambo*).

Nineteen ninety-three was the year in which Fernando Trueba's nostalgic sex comedy *Belle Epoque* won the Oscar for foreign-language film. But San Sebastián also marked the consecration of Almodóvar by a domestic film industry that had often marginalized him, in a special showing which brought together his first amateur super-8, *Folle, folle, fólleme, Tim* (Fuck, Fuck, Fuck Me, Tim) with rough-cut sequences of the as yet incomplete *Kika*.[5] If *Kika*, like Medem's *La ardilla roja*, was massacred by Spanish critics, still it grossed 500 million pesetas (around $5 million) in the domestic market.[6] And if Almodóvar complained loudly at the 'censorship' of his films enforced by the Motion Picture Association of America,[7] still *Kika* was in June 1994 the only foreign-language feature in the US top 30 box office grosses, taking over $1 million in 5 weeks.[8] *Fresa y chocolate* achieved similar commercial success in the US market, taking over $2 million in 16 weeks of release, boosted by an Oscar nomination.[9] Once more a homosexual theme proved no disadvantage to the niche marketing of small, foreign language films in the US; inversely, *La ardilla roja*'s revision of heterosexuality found no North American distributor.

Spanish–Cuban cultural relations were marked in the period by historical memory and identification, from the European side at least. *El País* spoke of Cubans' new desire to speak openly at 'the time of change' ('a la hora del cambio'), the word 'cambio' serving as a coded reminder to Spaniards of their own transition to democracy some twenty years earlier.[10] Another article criticizing the credulous Spanish reception of *Fresa y chocolate* accused Spaniards of believing that (like Spain under Franco) 'Cuba is different', an exceptional case undeserving of or inherently resistant to parliamentary democracy.[11] Some informal contacts between the two countries threw Alea's sexless vision of Cuban homosexuality into new light: crowded pages of contact ads in Spanish gay magazine *Men/Mensual* promised visitors a warm welcome from Havana youth, some of whom displayed their bodies in full-frontal photos with a defiant eroticism reminiscent of Arenas.[12]

This need not necessarily mean, however, that Anglo-American models of homosexual identity are at play here. And still we must pay attention to those who, like Arenas's master Virgilio Piñera, choose nomadism over the life of the queer tribe and silence over graphic self-expression. The problem with such a subtle and ironic position as Piñera's, often the only form of resistance to state terror, is that, as José Quiroga notes in his subtle reading of Piñera, it leaves heterosexual 'blindness' untouched.[13] It is a problem repeated in anthropological accounts of gay men and AIDS in Spain. Ironically, even IV drug users with AIDS now figure as a social type, readily identifiable to the HIV-negative public. Gay men with AIDS, however, typically choose privacy and thus do not register in the public sphere.[14] Yet if, as is still argued in the preface to a recent sociological study of gay men in the Spanish state, homosexuality has not yet become institutionalized there, and thus remains relatively invisible, still that study itself is written by a tenured university teacher.[15] The possibility of change is not to be ruled out. In Cuba, mirroring economic *apertura*, grey and grubby *Cine Cubano* changed in 1990 to a glossy, full-colour format, a revolution in visuals, if not in vision. And there was evidence of distorted traditions and new cultural connections: one cover showed a graphic work by Eisenstein, discreetly homo-erotic in tone;[16] a reprinted essay by Almodóvar advised Cuban filmmakers 'how to become an internationally renowned cineaste'.[17]

The persistence of invisibility and silence is not, however, of a strictly local character. Of the genres I have treated in this book, Sylvia Molloy has claimed autobiography as the writing of 'mortality' and 'masks', rather than a process of vital self-disclosure;[18] while Serge Daney has identified in documentary a 'fear of film', by which the image is thought to contaminate the purity of verbal narration.[19] The association of reproductive technology and mortality stretches back at least to André Bazin's *What Is Cinema?*, in which photography is compared to the embalming process of Egyptian mummification and singled out as the art which requires 'the absence of man'.[20] And if the 'fatal strategies' I have described in Spanish artists and intellectuals are not restricted to that country,[21] Pepe Espaliú's paradoxical practice of 'images that speak in silence'[22] remains exemplary in its rigour and resonance.

In his discussion of sexuality Freud was keen to distinguish between the psychological and the physiological: the disavowal of vision undertaken by the fetishist was not to be compared to an unperceived image striking the 'blind spot' of the retina;[23] the visual image in dreams, product of a regressive incarnation of an idea, was subject to complex processes of selective attraction and conditions of representability.[24] But it is the Freudian version of identification (a term I have ventured to use at various points in this book) which proves most fruitful in my argument. One extended discussion of this concept follows on from the analysis of the 'dream of the abandoned supper party'.[25] Here a 'clever woman' challenges Freud to show that the dream in which she attempted, but was unable, to arrange a dinner for friends, was indeed the fulfilment of a wish (as Freud had claimed of all dreams). Although the analysis is complex, it centres on the woman's identification with a thinner friend, whom she saw (unconsciously) as a rival for her husband's affections. Freud states that identification 'enables patients to suffer on behalf of a whole crowd of people' (p. 232); and that it 'is not simple imitation but assimilation on the basis of a similar aetiological pretension' (p. 233). It is just such an identification that is required of the spectator who confronts the representation of suffering in the cinema or art gallery, whether that suffering is inflicted by the state or illness: an identification which does not hysterically repeat the symptom, but comes to understand the causes (the aetiology) of the artistic and subjective process to which s/he is bearing witness. Of course, in Freud such identification is unconscious, even if it results in privileged knowledge (Freud notes that patients know more about each other than any doctor does). To render such a process conscious would be to confront the fear which had motivated the original repression, a fear which, according to Freud, 'express[es] a common sexual element' (p. 233). It might be something like, as in Vattimo, learning to dream, while knowing that one is dreaming. Or perhaps, as in Senel Paz's original story for *Fresa y chocolate*, giving a Lezamian supper party for a revolutionary apparatchik with 'penetrating eyes', a party which does not repress but rather celebrates the queer culinary tradition implicit in such an event.

Catherine Davies has argued for a similar expansive and sympathetic approach to identification in the case of Cuban cinema.[26] Directors such as Gutiérrez Alea attempted, as we saw, to take identification beyond narcissism and hysteria into the social sphere, in a way that would no longer simply reconfirm the status quo. While she and I would probably disagree over whether *Fresa y chocolate* achieves that laudable aim, we would agree that Cuba has reached a critical point at which 'the body politic can no longer be separated from waste': in *Fresa y chocolate* Diego tells us that Havana is collapsing into shit; in Daniel Díaz Torres's unsettling dystopia *Alicia en el pueblo de Maravillas* (Alice in Wondertown/in the Town of Maravillas, 1991) excrement is everywhere and council workers circle the town, throwing garbage into the street from trucks.[27] Such moments of border breakdown must prove profoundly disturbing in a society which once claimed to have integrated life, labour, and art.

In this book we have seen that the postwar politics or ethics of anti-illusionism, typified by *Cahiers du Cinéma* and the Cuban cinema of the 1960s, gave way during the 1980s to a generalized scepticism and irony, a postmodernism in Vattimo's sense, which spoke with a certain Latin accent. Thus while Almodóvar's *Entre tinieblas* (1983) was dismissed by *Variety* as of interest only to a youthful, domestic audience,[28] a decade later the marginal had become the mainstream and *Kika*, shown around the world, tilted quixotically against the excesses of Spanish television. Or again, Almendros's low-budget documentary on gays in Cuba gave way to a major feature on the same theme by Cuba's best-known director, which proved to be one of the most successful films ever made in that country. There was also a certain return to referentiality, however ironized, suspended or bracketed: Almodóvar, Arenas and Espaliú, each in his very different way, bear witness to the persistence of subjectivity and of solidarity, which (like de Lauretis's version of sexual difference) 'cling like a wet silk dress'. If it is still an urgent priority to refute the unacknowledged standard of vision or ocularcentrism which has proved mortally dangerous to lesbians, gay men and PWAs, then we must also work towards an accommodation with truth and testimony. But a third way between the graphic excesses of Almodóvar and Medem and the ironic aesthetic of disappearance of Espaliú is not to be found in *Fresa y chocolate*'s reprise of bourgeois realism. Perhaps it occurs rather in the oscillation of Arenas's writings, taken as a whole, as they hesitate between autobiography and fiction, truth and fabulation. There may well be no way out of the vision machine; certainly there is no space innocent of technology. But freed from rigid and repressive Anglo-Saxon modernity, Spanish and Cuban film and literature offer us images that speak to us eloquently even as they keep their silence.

NOTES

1 Miguel Juan Payán, *El cine español de los 90* (Madrid: JC, 1993), p. 45.

2 John Hopewell, *El cine español después de Franco* (Madrid: El Arquero, 1989), p. 463.

3 Ferrán Alberich, *Cuatro años de cine español* (Madrid: Comunidad, 1991), p. 206. *Bernarda Alba* made 74 million pesetas; the biggest grossing film in the four-year period, Almodóvar's *Mujeres al borde de un ataque de nervios* (Women on the Verge of a Nervous Breakdown), made 974 million.

4 *Moving Pictures* 153 (16 September 1993), p. 17.

5 Maruja Torres, 'Pedro Almodóvar: "No me quiero morir nunca"', *El País* (25 September 1993), p. 22.

6 Anon., '495 millones de recaudación', *El País* (4 May 1994).

7 Andrés F. Rubio, 'Almodóvar ataca el sistema censor de EE UU en la presentación de *Kika* en Nueva York', *El País* (4 May 1994).

8 *Screen International* (10 June 1994), p. 33.

9 *Variety* (15–21 May 1995), p. 24.

10 'Desesperados: hablan los cubanos a la hora del cambio', *El País Semanal* (9 October 1994).

11 Antonio Elorza, 'Sabores de un helado', *El País* (26 May 1994).

12 Oreste and Shenko, students majoring in sport, offer cheap accommodation and an introduction service ('facilidad de relación'), *Men/Mensual* 53 (1995), p. 64. The ads from Cubans in this magazine, whether overtly sexual or sweetly romantic in tone, far outnumber those from all other countries combined.

13 José Quiriga, 'Fleshing Out Virgilio Piñera from the Cuban Closet', in Emilie Bergmann and Paul Julian Smith, eds, *¿Entiendes?: Queer Readings, Hispanic Texts*, (Durham, NC: Duke University Press, 1995), p. 177.

14 Juan F. Gamella, 'The Spread of Intravenous Drug Use and AIDS in a Neighbourhood in Spain', *Medical Anthropology Quarterly* 8.2 (1994), p. 149.

15 I cite the introduction by Jesús M. de Miguel to Oscar Guasch, *La sociedad rosa* (Barcelona: Anagrama, 1991), pp. 13, 15.

16 *Cine Cubano* 138 (1993).

17 'Consejos para llegar a ser un cineasta de fama internacional', *Cine Cubano* 134 (1992), pp. 58–64.

18 Sylvia Molloy, *At Face Value: Autobiographical Writing in Spanish America* (Cambridge: Cambridge University Press, 1991), p. 1.

19 Serge Daney, in his review of Jean Aurel's *Staline*, in *Ciné journal* (Paris: Cahiers du Cinéma, 1986), p. 80.

20 André Bazin, *What Is Cinema?*, trans. Hugh Gray (Berkeley: University of California Press, 1967), pp. 9, 11.

21 Similar strategies recur in some art works from Australia and the US; see Ted Gott, ed., *Don't Leave Me This Way: Art in the Age of AIDS* (Melbourne, London and New York: Thames and Hudson, 1994).

22 I take the phrase from the exhibition note in *Pasajes* (Seville: Expo, 1992), p. 74.

23 Sigmund Freud, 'Fetishism', in *On Sexuality* (Harmondsworth: Penguin, 1977), p. 353.

24 Sigmund Freud, *The Interpretation of Dreams* (Harmondsworth: Penguin, 1986), p. 699.

25 *The Interpretation of Dreams*, pp. 228–33.

26 Catherine Davies, 'Identification and Interpretation in Cuban Cinema of the 1980s and 1990s', unpublished paper.

27 *Alicia* was banned after its release; see *Cine Cubano* 135 (1992), pp. 16–22 for an account of the controversy and reprinted reviews from Cuban magazines; in an interview with Mario Benedetti, Alfredo Guevara, incoming head of ICAIC, claimed to know nothing of the affair; 'La hazaña cubana de empezar de nuevo', *Cine Cubano* 139 (1993), pp. 49–51.

28 Peter Besas, *Variety* (15 May 1984).

FILMOGRAPHIES

1 *La casa de Bernarda Alba* (The House of Bernarda Alba), Spain 1987, director Mario Camus (see chapter 1).

Production company	Paraíso Films; in collaboration with TVE
Executive producers	Jaime Borell, José Miguel Juárez, Antonio Oliver
Production manager	Juan de la Flor
Screenplay	Mario Camus, Antonio Larreta; based on the play by Federico García Lorca
Director of photography	Fernando Arribas
Editor	José M. Biurrun
Graphic design	Daniel Gil
Costume design	Pepe Rubio
Sound	Bernardo Menz

103 mins

CAST

Irene Gutiérrez Caba	Bernarda
Ana Belén	Adela
Victoria Peña	Martirio

Florinda Chico	La Poncia
Enriqueta Carbelleira	Angustias
Merced Lezcano	Amelia
Rosario García Ortega	María Josefa

Having buried her husband, Bernard Alba, a figure of wealth and consequence in the village, returns to the house where her senile mother is kept confined largely to the attic. Ignoring the warnings of her trusted servant La Poncia, Bernarda announces an eight-year period of strict mourning during which her five unmarried daughters – Angustias, Martirio, Magdalena, Amelia, and Adela – will not be permitted to leave the house. Frustration flares into resentment when the sisters learn that Angustias, the eldest at thirty-nine, is to be allowed to entertain a suitor for her hand. Martirio, particularly embittered because Bernarda has swiftly terminated her own 'unsuitable' romance with a farmer's son, consoles herself with the knowledge that the spinsterish Angustias – only child of Bernarda's first husband, and commanding a much larger dowry than her sisters – is being wooed by handsome, 25-year-old Pepe el Romano only because of her money. But it is the secretive Adela, already enamoured of Pepe, who takes action, despite a cautionary scene witnessed by the household: an unmarried girl who allegedly killed her baby is pursued and lynched by villagers in the street outside. Undeterred, Adela starts waylaying Pepe after his authorized evening visits to Angustias, eventually making love with him in the stables. Spying on the lovers, unable to contain her jealousy, Martirio summons her mother. Adela is defiant; Pepe bolts in the confusion; and Bernarda, firing two wild shots after him as he flees, announces that he is dead. Defying her mother, the repentant Martirio insists that Pepe got away. Locking herself in her room, Adela nevertheless hangs herself. Bernarda orders that the body be cut down and dressed as a virgin, so that no rumours of shame will be voiced. *Tom Milne*[1]

2 *Entre tinieblas* (Dark Habits), Spain 1983, director Pedro Almodóvar (see chapter 1).

Production company	Tesauro
Producer	Luis Calvo
Production manager	Luis Briales

Screenplay	Pedro Almodóvar
Director of photography	Angel Luis Fernández
Editor	José Salcedo
Production design	Pin Morales
	Román Arango
Costume design (Yolanda and the Virgins)	Francis Montesinos
Sound editors	Martin Müller
	Armin Fausten

115 mins

CAST

Cristina S. Pascual	Yolanda
Julieta Serrano	Mother Superior
Mari Carrillo	Marquesa
Marisa Paredes	Sister Manure
Chus Lampreave	Sister Rat
Carmen Maura	Sister Damned
Lina Canalejas	Sister Snake
Manuel Zarzo	Chaplain

Madrid. Yolanda Bell, a singer and part-time heroin dealer-cum-addict whose boyfriend has just died of a mysterious overdose, is on the run from the police. She takes refuge in a convent run by the Humble Redeemers, a small order of nuns who purportedly do charitable work with the 'fallen'. Following the recent death of an aristocrat who supported the order because his daughter Virginia – who went to Africa as a missionary and was eaten by cannibals – belonged to it, his widow, the Marquesa, has withdrawn their funding. The Mother Superior, a heroin user and sentimental lesbian, is struggling to keep the convent going. Yolanda meets the other nuns: Sister Rat, who writes sensationalist novels under a pseudonym, drawing on the experiences of 'fallen' women; Sister Damned, who is devoted to a tiger she has raised from a cub; Sister Manure, an acid casualty; and Sister Snake, a fashion designer who has fallen in love with a priest.

A letter arrives from Africa for the Mother Superior, containing information about Virginia which she tries to sell to the Marquesa.

In honour of the Mother Superior, and expecting a visit from their mother order, the nuns throw a party at which Yolanda agrees to sing. Yolanda, who has become friendly with the Mother Superior and cured her drug habit, betrays her by helping the Marquesa to find the letter, which reveals that Virginia died after giving birth to a son, who has been reared in the jungle by apes. Yolanda sings, scandalizing the visiting nuns, who insist that the order be disbanded. Yolanda leaves, and most of the sisters drift away, leaving the Mother Superior devastated. *Kim Newman*[2]

3 *Kika*, Spain 1993, director Pedro Almodóvar (see chapter 2)

Production company	El Deseo S. A. and Ciby 2000
Executive producer	Agustín Almodóvar
Production manager	Alejandro Vázquez
Screenplay	Pedro Almodóvar
Director of photography	Alfredo Mayo
Editor	José Salcedo
Set design	Javier Fernández
	Alain Bainée
Costume design	Jean-Paul Gaultier
	José María Cossío
	Gianni Versace
Sound	Jean-Paul Mugel

114 mins

CAST

Verónica Forqué	Kika
Peter Coyote	Nicholas
Victoria Abril	Andrea Caracortada
Alex Casanovas	Ramón
Rossy de Palma	Juana
Santiago Lajusticia	Pablo
Anabel Alonso	Amparo
Bibi Andersen	Susana
Charo López	Ramón's mother

Kika is an ever-optimistic beautician living with Ramón, an

introspective and uncommunicative underwear photographer she met when summoned to make up his cataleptic 'corpse'. Returning from abroad, Ramón's stepfather, American novelist Nicholas Pearce, moves into the flat above. Ramón and Nicholas jointly own a country house ('Youkali') bequeathed to them by Ramón's mother , with whom Ramón has been obsessed since her suicide. Unsatisfied by her relationship with Ramón, Kika secretly enjoys occasional sex with the mysterious and seductive Nicholas.

Ramón also has his secrets: before Kika, he had been involved with Andrea Caracortada ('Scarface'), an ex-psychologist turned crime reporter. Their relationship ended dramatically, leaving Andrea with a sizeable grudge and a scar on her face. Equipped with a motorbike and customized black rubber suit, Andrea specializes in on-the-spot crime reports and sensationalist interviews with victims and perpetrators for her TV reality show 'The Worst of the Day'.

Andrea encounters Kika when pursuing mentally deficient convicted rapist Pablo, who escaped while on parole from prison to attend a religious festival in his home village. Unknown to Kika, her maid Juana is Pablo's sister and Kika's flat is his first port of call on the run. Juana, a plain-speaking lesbian who is in love with Kika, does her best to protect her sleeping mistress from Pablo's voracious sexual appetite by promising to satisfy his needs herself. She decides to send Pablo into hiding and tells him to steal some of Ramón's cameras, concealing her role in the theft by getting Pablo to slug her and tie her to a chair. While Juana is bound and unconscious, Pablo repeatedly rapes Kika until the police arrive and pull him away. He escapes as Andrea arrives on the scene. Kika angrily refuses to answer Andrea's intrusive questions and tries to put the incident behind her, only to be further humiliated by the TV screening of a video recording of the rape sent in by a neighbouring voyeur. Discovering that Ramón is the source of the video, she moves out.

Andrea's continuing scrutiny of Ramón's video and Nicholas' latest manuscript lead her to suspect Nicholas of multiple murder and, desperate for the scoop, she pursues him to Youkali, where Ramón has already discovered a dead body and confronted him with the evidence of his mother's murder. While Ramón lies in another cataleptic swoon, Andrea forces her way in and dies in a struggle with Nicholas. Kika, drawn by a letter from Ramón, turns up in time to hear Nicholas' dying confession and revive Ramón.

Following the ambulance taking him to hospital, however, she picks up a hitcher, with whom she drives off into the sunset. *Rikki Morgan*[3]

4 *Mauvaise conduite* (Improper Conduct), France 1983, directors Néstor Almendros and Orlando Jiménez Leal (see chapter 3).

Production company	Films du Losange; Antenne 2
Producers	Margaret Menegoz
	Barbet Schroeder
	Michel Thoulouze
Production supervisor	Luis Argueta
Production manager	Nicole Flipo
Research	Carlos Ripoll
	Frédérick Epin
Photography	Dominique Merlin
Editors	Michel Pion
	Alain Tortevoix
Sound recording	Daniel Delmau
	Phil Pearl
	Norman Koppelman

114 mins

On-screen participants

Lorenzo Monreal, Jorge Lago, Julio Medina, César Bermudez, José Mario, Rafael de Palet, Jorge Ronet, Héctor Aldao, Jaime Bellechasse, Mireya Robles, Luis Lazo, Caracol, Reinaldo Arenas, Juan Abreu, Gilberto Ruiz, Juan Matín, Félix Hernández, Elaine del Castillo, Reinaldo García Ramos, Heberto Padilla, Guillermo Cabrera Infante, Carlos Franqui, Juan Goytisolo, Fidel Castro, Susan Sontag, Armando Valladares, Ana María Simo, Martha Frayde, René Ariza.

A documentary on human rights in Cuba, opening with archive footage of a 1966 press conference in which dancers from the Cuban National Ballet Company announce their defection in Paris. Twenty-eight other exiles then explain why they also left Cuba. Their accounts are focused on experiences in the 1960s of UMAP detention camps (which held homosexuals amongst

others) and on the *Mariel* exodus of 1980, when the suspension of
US immigration quotas allowed thousands of Cubans to gain
admission to the United states. These interviews are counterpointed with excerpts from archive interviews with Fidel Castro.
Jane Root[4]

5 *Fresa y chocolate* (Strawberry and Chocolate), Cuba 1993, directors Tomás Gutiérrez Alea and Juan Carlos Tabío (see chapter 4).

Production company	ICAIC; Instituto Mejicano de Cinematografía; Telemadrid
Executive producers	Camilo Vives
	Frank Cabrera
	Georgina Balzaretti
Production manager	Miguel Mendoza
Screenplay	Senel Paz, based on his story *El lobo, el bosque, y el hombre nuevo* (The Wolf, the Forest, and the New Man)
Director of photography	Mario García Joya
Editors	Rolando Martínez
	Miriam Talavera
	Osvaldo Donatien
Set decorator	Orlando González
Costume design	Miriam Dueñas
Sound	Germinal Hernández
Music	José María Vitier

111 mins

CAST

Jorge Perugorría	Diego
Vladimir Cruz	David
Mirta Ibarra	Nancy
Francisco Gattorno	Miguel
Joel Angelino	Germán
Marilyn Solaya	Vivian
Andrés Cortina	Santería priest

David, a student at Havana University, takes his girlfriend Vivian to a cheap hotel, but seeing her tears declares he won't sleep with her until they are married. He is devastated when she marries someone else. At a cafe he meets a gay artist, Diego, who takes him back to his apartment on the pretext of showing David some photographs. At the flat David sees religious statues made by Diego's friend Germán; Diego explains he plans to mount an exhibition of them with the help of a foreign embassy. At once intrigued and repelled by Diego's conversation, David recounts the experience to his fellow student Miguel, who tells him to keep up his contacts with this potential subversive.

Discontented in her marriage, Vivian invites David to become her lover, but he refuses. Visiting Diego again, he is introduced to Cuban culture and Scotch whisky, and also meets his neighbour Nancy, the Neighbourhood Watch officer for Diego's apartment block. When she attempts suicide, David helps Diego get her to hospital and donates blood for her. Though still wary of Diego's homosexuality, David is increasingly drawn to his cultured life-style, and his own suppressed ambition to write is rekindled.

Germán's exhibition is banned; furious, he smashes his own work. Despite David's warnings, Diego sends a letter of protest to the Cuban authorities. Nancy, attracted to David and learning he is a virgin, resolves to initiate him. After dinner at the apartment, Diego leaves David and Nancy alone together and they make love. Miguel, believing David has been corrupted, visits Diego and attacks him, but David intervenes. Under pressure to leave Cuba, Diego and David say farewell – and embrace for the first time.
Philip Kemp[5]

6 *La ardilla roja* (The Red Squirrel), Spain 1993, director Julio Medem (see chapter 6).

Production company	Sogetel
Executive producer	Fernando de Garcillán
Executive in charge of production	Ricardo García Arroja
Coproducer	Lola Pérez
Production manager	Luis Gutiérrez
Screenplay	Julio Medem
Director of photography	Gonzalo Fernández Berridi
Editor	María Elena Sainz de Rozas

Art Director	Alvaro Machimbarrena
Set decorator	Satur Idarreta
Wardrobe	María Isabel Gutiérrez
Sound recordist	Julio Recuero
Music	Alberto Iglesias

104 mins

CAST

Nancho Novo	Jota
Emma Suárez	Lisa
María Barranco	Carmen
Carmelo Gómez	Félix
Karra Elejalde	Antón
Cristina Marcos	Girl with Blue Hair
Mónica Molina	Girl with Red Hair

Jota, a failed rock musician deserted by his girlfriend, is contemplating suicide one night by the sea in his native San Sebastián. Suddenly a motorbike crashes on to the beach. Accompanying its shocked rider to the hospital, Jota claims that he is her boyfriend. Claiming to have lost her memory, 'Lisa' (as Jota has named her) rides off with Jota to a camp site on the edge of a reservoir. It is called 'The Red Squirrel' after the notoriously shy animal that lives in the forest there. The new couple meet a vacationing family with whom they become friendly: *machista* taxi driver Antón, brow-beaten housewife Carmen and their precocious son and daughter. When the boy hypnotizes Lisa, Jota learns that she is really 'Sofía', and is fleeing from her psychotic husband Félix. Both Jota and Lisa take advantage of her amnesia to invent fantasies about themselves and each other.

After they become romantically involved, Jota and Lisa hear a radio announcement placed by Félix asking for news of her whereabouts. Notified by the taxi driver, Félix arrives and challenges Jota, cutting off his own cheek to show his devotion to his wife. Lisa/Sofía flees on her motorbike; the two men follow in Félix's car (he is a notorious hit-and-run driver). When it plunges into the reservoir, Jota escapes but Félix drowns. Jota discovers that the hospital orderly to whom he had given invented details of Lisa's identity at the start of the film is in fact Sofía's brother. Through him he tracks her down to the squirrel enclosure in the Madrid zoo. They embrace. *Paul Julian Smith*[6]

NOTES

1 *Monthly Film Bulletin* (March 1990).

2 *Monthly Film Bulletin* (October 1990).

3 *Sight and Sound* (July 1994).

4 *Monthly Film Bulletin* (July 1985).

5 *Sight and Sound* (September 1994).

6 *Sight and Sound* (October 1994).

BIBLIOGRAPHY

Aggleton, Peter et al., eds, *AIDS: Social Representations, Social Practices* (New York: Falmer, 1989).

Alas, Leopoldo, *La acera de enfrente* (Madrid: El Papagayo, 1994).

Alberich, Ferrán, *Cuatro años de cine español* (Madrid: Comunidad, 1991).

Aliaga, Juan Vicente,'Once imágenes del tiempo: El Nido', *El Europeo* (Winter 1993–4).

——, 'Speak to Me, Body: An Approach to the Work of Pepe Espaliú', in *Pepe Espaliú: 1986–93* (Seville: Junta de Andalucía, 1994).

—— and José Miguel G. Cortés, *De amor y rabia: acerca del arte y el SIDA* (Valencia: Universidad Politécnica de Valencia, 1993).

Almendros, Néstor, 'Improper Conduct', *American Film*, vol. 9, no. 10 (September 1984), pp. 18, 70–1.

——, *Man with A Camera* (London: Faber, 1984).

——, 'Almendros and Documentary', *Sight and Sound*, vol. 55, no. 1 (Winter 1985–6), pp. 50–4.

——, *Cinemanía* (Barcelona: Seix Barral, 1992).

—— and Orlando Jiménez Leal, *Conducta impropia* (Madrid: Playor, 1984).

Almodóvar, Pedro, 'The Pain in Spain', *Time Out* [London] (10–17 May 1995), p. 74.

Anonymous, 'Néstor Almendros gana el premio del Festival de Cine de Derechos Humanos de Estrasburgo', *Cineinforme* 130 (May 1984), p. 9.

Arenas, Reinaldo, *El mundo alucinante* (Mexico: Diógenes, 1978).

——, *Arturo, la estrella más brillante* (Barcelona: Montesinos, 1984).

——, *La loma del ángel* (Barcelona: Dador, 1989).

——, *Voluntad de vivir manifestándose* (Madrid: Betania, 1989).

——, *Viaje a la Habana* (Miami: Universal, 1990).

——, *Antes que anochezca* (Barcelona: Tusquets, 1992).

—— and Jorge Camacho, *Un plebiscito a Fidel Castro* (Madrid: Betania, 1990).

Bad Object Choices [sic], eds, *How Do I Look?: Queer Film and Video* (Seattle: Bay Press, 1991).

Barnard, Timothy, 'Death Is Not True', in John King, Ana M. López and Manuel Alvarado, eds, *Mediating Two Worlds: Cinematic Encounters in the Americas* (London: BFI, 1993), pp. 230–41.

Baudrillard, Jean, *Selected Writings*, Mark Poster, ed. (Cambridge: Polity, 1988).

Bazin, André, *What is Cinema?*, trans. Hugh Gray (Berkeley: University of California Press, 1967).

Bejel, Emilio, 'Senel Paz: homosexualidad, nacionalismo, y utopía', *Plural* 269 (February 1994), pp. 58–65.

Benedetti, Mario, 'La hazaña cubana de empezar de nuevo' [interview with Alfredo Guevara], *Cine Cubano* 139 (1993), pp. 49–51.

Bergmann, Emilie and Paul Julian Smith, eds, *¿Entiendes?: Queer Readings, Hispanic Texts* (Durham, NC: Duke University Press, 1995).

Besas, Peter, review of *Entre tinieblas*, *Variety* (15 May 1984).

——, review of *La ardilla roja*, *Variety* (10 May 1993), p. 238.

Blanch, Teresa, '1982–92: Spain at the Beginning of a Well Defined Intersection', in *Pasajes: Spanish Art Today* (Seville: Electa, 1992), pp. 23–32.

Borkowski, Mark, press release for *Kika* (London, 9 June 1994).

Bojstad, Anneli, review of *La ardilla roja*, *Screen International* 905 (30 April 1993), p. 16.

Cabrera Infante, Guillermo, 'Cuba's Shadow', *Film Comment*, vol. 24, no. 3 (May/June 1985), pp. 43–5.

Cardín, Alberto, *Como si nada* (Valencia: Pre-textos, 1981).

——, *Despojos* (Valencia: Pre-textos, 1981).

——, *SIDA: ¿Maldición bíblica o enfermedad letal?* (Barcelona: Laertes, 1985).

——, *Detrás por delante* (Barcelona: Laertes, 1986).

——, *Lo próximo y lo ajeno* (Barcelona: Icaria, 1990).

——, *Dialéctica y canibalismo* (Bellaterra: Universitat Autònoma de Barcelona, 1991).

——, *SIDA: Enfoques alternativos* (Barcelona: Laertes, 1991).

Carver, Benedict, 'A Cheerful Recession', *Sight and Sound* (January 1994), p. 10.

Celemenski, Michel, review of *Mauvaise conduite*, *Cinématographe* 98 (March 1984), pp. 27–8.

Chanan, Michael, *The Cuban Image* (London: BFI, 1985).

Charity, Tom, 'Basque in Glory' [interview with Julio Medem], *Time Out* [London] (28 September–5 October 1994), p. 18.

Cine Cubano (1983–93) (Havana: ICAIC).

Clot, Manel, 'Once imágenes del tiempo: Carriying I' [sic], *El Europeo* (Winter 1993–4).

——, 'Dos palabras sobre el amor (Una idea del desastre)', in *Pepe Espaliú: 10 de febrero–4 de abril de 1994* (Madrid: Museo Nacional Centro de Arte Reina Sofía, 1994), unpaginated.

Crimp, Douglas and Adam Rolston, *Aids Demo Graphics* (Seattle: Bay Press, 1990).

Cubitt, Sean, review of *Improper Conduct*, *City Limits* [London] 171 (11 January 1985), p. 23.

——, 'Cuba libre?' [interview with Michael Chanan], *City Limits* [London] 171 (11 January 1985), p. 14.

Daney, Serge, *La Rampe: cahier critique 1970–82* (Paris: Cahiers du Cinéma/Gallimard, 1983).

——, *Ciné journal* (Paris: Cahiers du Cinéma, 1986).

——, *Le Salaire du zappeur* (Paris: Ramsay, 1988).

——, 'Falling Out of Love', *Sight and Sound* 2.3 (1992), pp. 14–16.

——, 'Film Buff on a Journey' [undated text reproduced for second annual Serge Daney Lecture at 23rd Rotterdam Film Festival].

—— and Jean-Pierre Oudart, 'Travail, lecture, jouissance', *Cahiers du Cinéma* 222 (July 1970), pp. 39–51.

——, 'The Name of the Author (on the "Place" of Death in Venice)', in *Cahiers du Cinéma: Volume 3: 1969–72 The Politics of Representation*, Nick Browne, ed. (London: Routledge/BFI, 1990), pp. 307–24.

Davies, Catherine, 'Identification and Interpretation in Cuban Cinema of the 1980s and 1990s', unpublished paper.

de Lauretis, Teresa, *Technologies of Gender: Essays on Theory, Film, and Fiction* (London: Macmillan, 1987).

——, 'Sexual Indifference and Lesbian Representation', *Theater Journal* 40 (1988), pp. 155–77.

——, 'Film and the Visible', in Bad Object Choices [sic], eds, *How Do I Look?: Queer Film and Video* (Seattle: Bay Press, 1991), pp. 223–64.

Deleuze, Gilles, 'Optimisme, pessimisme, et voyage', in Serge Daney, *Ciné journal* (Paris: Cahiers du Cinéma, 1986), pp. 5–13.

de Miguel, Jesús M. and David L. Kirp, 'Spain: An Epidemic of Denial', in David L. Kirp and Ronald Bayer, eds, *AIDS in the Industrialized Democracies* (New Brunswick: Rutgers University Press, 1992), pp. 168–84.

de Ros, Xon, '*Vacas* and Basque Cinema: The Making of a Tradition', unpublished paper.

de Villaleriga, Isabel, 'Emma Suárez', *La Vanguardia* [magazine] (November 1988).

Dmytryk, Edward, *On Film Editing* (Boston and London: Focal, 1984).

——, *On Screen Writing* (Boston and London: Focal, 1985).

Edelman, Lee, 'The Mirror and the Tank: "AIDS", Subjectivity, and the Rhetoric of Activism', in Timothy F. Murphy and Suzanne Poirier, eds, *Writing AIDS: Gay Literature, Language, and Analysis* (New York: Columbia University Press, 1993), pp. 9–38.

El Deseo, S. A., *Kika: un film de Almodóvar* [pressbook] (1993).

Elorza, Antonio, 'Sabores de un helado' [on *Fresa y chocolate*], *El País* (26 May 1994).

¿Entiendes? (1991–4) (Madrid: Comunidad Gay de Madrid).

Espaliú, Pepe, *En estos cinco años* (Madrid: Estampa, 1993).

Evora, José Antonio, 'Díos nos perdone; digo, Diego, en su nombre', in *Tomás Gutiérrez Alea: poesía y revolución* (Filmoteca Canaria, 1994), pp. 203–12.

Fernández Cifuentes, Luis, review of Gibson, *Federico García Lorca*, *Nueva Revista de Filología* 34 (1985–6), pp. 224–32.

Fernández Santos, Angel, review of *Kika*, *El País* (6 November 1993).

Ferrando, Carlos, 'Emma Suárez, una niña bien para José Coronado', *Diario 16* (27 August 1990).

Freud, Sigmund, *On Sexuality* (Harmondsworth: Penguin, 1977).

——, *The Interpretation of Dreams* (Harmondsworth: Penguin, 1986).

Fuentes, Víctor, 'El cine de Almodóvar y la posmodernidad española (logros y límites)', in George Cabello Castellet, Jaume Martí-Olivella and Guy H. Wood, eds, *Cine-Lit: Essays on Peninsular Film and Fiction* (Corvallis/Portland: Oregon State/Portland State/Reed College, 1992), pp. 209–18.

Gamella, Juan F., 'The Spread of Intravenous Drug Use and AIDS in a Neighbourhood in Spain', *Medical Anthropology Quarterly* 8.2 (1994), pp. 131–60.

García, Rocío, 'Roca y Carmen Alborch acuerdan la paz en el conflicto sobre el cine catalán', *El País* (9 February 1994).

——, 'El mecenazgo cuenta por fin con un marco legal, *El País* (4 November 1994).

García Lorca, Federico, *La casa de Bernarda Alba*, H. Ramsden, ed. (Manchester: Manchester University press, 1983).

Gibson, Ian, *Federico García Lorca: A Life* (London: Faber, 1989).

Gilman, Sander, 'Plague in Germany 1939/1989: Cultural Images of Race, Space, and Disease', in Timothy F. Murphy and Suzanne Poirier, eds, *Writing AIDS: Gay Literature, Language, and Analysis* (New York: Columbia University Press, 1993).

Gott, Ted, ed., *Don't Leave Me This Way: Art in the Age of AIDS* (Melbourne, London and New York: Thames and Hudson, 1995).

Grant, Simon, 'Pepe Espaliú', *Art Monthly* (April 1994), p. 175.

Guasch, Oscar, *La sociedad rosa* (Barcelona: Anagrama, 1991).

Gutiérrez Alea, Tomás, *Memories of Underdevelopment*, introduced by Michael Chanan (New Brunswick and London: Rutgers University Press, no date given).

——, 'Dialéctica del espectador', in *Poesía y revolución* (Filmoteca Canaria, 1994), pp. 33–133.

Haraway, Donna J., *Simians, Cyborgs, and Women* (London: Free Association, 1991).

Haro Ibars, Eduardo, *Gay Rock* (Madrid: Júcar, 1975).

——, *Intersecciones* (Libertarias/Prodhufi, 1991).

Hauge, Michael, *Writing Screenplays That Sell* (New York: Harper, 1991).

Heredero, Carlos F., *Las huellas del tiempo: cine español 1951–61* (Madrid: Filmoteca, 1993).

Hocquenghem, Guy, *Homosexual Desire* (London: Allison & Busby, 1978).

'Hitch.', review of *Improper Conduct*, *Variety* (25 April 1984).

Holguín, Antonio, *Pedro Almodóvar* (Madrid: Cátedra, 1994).

Hooper, John, *The Spaniards* (London: Penguin, 1987).

——, *The New Spaniards* (London: Penguin, 1995).

Hopewell, John, *Out of the Past: Spanish Cinema After Franco* (London: BFI, 1986).

——, *El cine español después de Franco* (Madrid: El Arquero, 1989).

——, 'Look through Spanish Eyes', *Moving Pictures* (18 November 1993), p. 12.

——, 'Spotlight: Cannes Preview: Spain', *Variety* (15–21 May 1995), pp. C15, C38.

International Federation of Film Archives, *International Directory of Cinematographers, Set and Costume Designers in Film: Volume 12: Cuba (From the Beginnings to 1990)*, Alfred Krautz, ed., Lourdes Castro Ramos, coordinator (Munich, London, New York, Paris: K. G. Saur, 1992).

Jay, Martin, 'In the Empire of the Gaze: Foucault and the Denigration of Vision in Twentieth-Century French Thought', in David Couzens Hoy, ed., *Foucault: A Critical Reader* (Oxford: Blackwell, 1986), pp. 175–204.

King, John, *Magical Reels: A History of Cinema in Latin America* (London : Verso, 1990).

——, Ana M. López and Manuel Alvarado, eds, *Mediating Two Worlds: Cinematic Encounters in the Americas* (London: BFI, 1993).

Kirp, David L. and Ronald Bayer, eds, *AIDS in the Industrialized Democracies* (New Brunswick: Rutgers University Press, 1992).

Llinás, Francisco, *Directores de fotografía del cine español* (Madrid: Filmoteca Española, 1989).

Llovet, Ana, '"La salud no te la devuelven": los afectados por el aceite de colza contemplan con cautela el posible cobro de las indemniza-ciones', *El País* (1 September 1994).

London Film Festival, *Official Programme: 31st London Film Festival* (London: BFI, 1987).

López, Ana M., 'Cuban Cinema in Exile: The "Other" Island', *Jump Cut* 38 (1993), pp. 51–9.

López Echevarrieta, Alberto, *Cine vasco: ¿realidad o ficción?* (Bilbao: Mensajero, no date).

Lorenci, Miguel, 'El Museo Reina Sofía rinde un homenaje póstumo a Pepe Espaliú', *Ya* (11 February 1994).

Lorenzo, Ricardo and Héctor Anabitarte, *Sida: el asunto está que arde* (Madrid: Revolución, 1987).

Lupton, Deborah, *Moral Threats and Dangerous Desires: AIDS in the News Media* (London: Taylor and Francis, 1994).

Mann, Jonathan et al., eds, *AIDS in the World* (Cambridge, MA and London: Harvard University Press, 1992).

Marinero, Francisco, review of *Entre tinieblas*, *Diario 16* (8 October 1983).

——, review of *Vacas*, *El Mundo* (6–12 March 1992).

Martínez Ten, Pilar, *La mujer y el SIDA* (Madrid: Instituto de la Mujer, 1992).

'M. C.', review of *Mauvaise conduite*, *Positif* 279 (May 1984), pp. 72–3.

Merck, Mandy, 'The Train of Thought in Freud's "Case of Homosexuality in a Woman"', in *Perversions: Deviant Readings* (London: Virago, 1993), pp. 13–32.

Ministerio de Salud y Consumo (Plan Nacional sobre el SIDA), *Actitudes Sociales ante el SIDA: informe de resultados, población general* (Madrid: MSC, 1990).

Mirabet i Mullol, Antoni, *Funció de les organitzacions no governmentals de servei en SIDA* (Barcelona: Associació SIDA-STUDI, 1992).

Moix, Terenci, 'Mi Néstor Almendros', *El País* (7 March 1992), p. 11.

——, *Suspiros de España: la copla y el cine de nuestro recuerdo* (Barcelona: Plaza y Janés, 1993).

Molina Foix, Vicente, *El cine estilográfico* (Barcelona: Anagrama, 1993).

Molloy, Sylvia, *At Face Value: Autobiographical Writing in Spanish America* (Cambridge: Cambridge University Press, 1991).

Monterde, José Enrique, *Veinte años de cine español: un cine bajo la paradoja* (Barcelona: Paidós, 1993).

Morgan, Ricky, review of *Kika*, *Sight and Sound* (July 1994), p. 48.

Moving Pictures [five special issues for San Sebastián film festival] (September 1993).

Mujika, L. M., *Historia de la literatura euskerika* (San Sebastián: Haranburu, 1979).

Muñoz, Diego, 'Emma Suárez: el éxito de una actriz "maldita"', *El País* (25 September 1990).

——, 'Julio Medem pasa del campo al cámping: el director de *Vacas* rueda *La ardilla roja*', *El País* (5 October 1992).

Murphy, Timothy F. and Suzanne Poirier, eds, *Writing AIDS: Gay Literature, Language, and Analysis* (New York: Columbia University Press, 1993).

Navarrete, Luis, 'Muere el diseñador Manuel Piña, víctima del SIDA', *El País* (9 October 1994).

Oppenheimer, Walter, 'El Parlamento Europeo defiende la igualdad legal para los homosexuales', *El País* (9 February 1994).

Paranagua, Paulo Antonio, ed., *Le Cinéma cubain* (Paris: Centre Pompidou, 1990).

Parker, Richard, *Sexuality, Politics, and AIDS in Brazil: In Another World?* (London and Washington DC: Falmer, 1993).

Patton, Cindy, *Inventing AIDS* (New York and London: Routledge, 1990).

Payán, Miguel Juan, *El cine español de los 90* (Madrid: JC, 1993).

Paz, Senel, *El lobo, el bosque, y el hombre nuevo* (Mexico: Era, 1991).

Quintana, Angel, 'Violència y bogeria vistes per unes vaques' [review of *Vacas*], *Punt* [Gerona] (30 May 1992).

Quiroga, José, 'Fleshing Out Virgilio Piñera from the Cuban Closet', in *¿Entiendes?: Queer Readings, Hispanic Texts*, Emilie Bergmann and Paul Julian Smith, eds, (Durham, NC: Duke University Press, 1995), pp. 168–80.

Rich, B. Ruby, 'Bay of Pix', *American Film*, vol. 9, no. 9, (July/August 1984), pp. 57–9.

Robaina, Tomás, 'Carta acerca de *Antes que anochezca*, autobiografía de Reinaldo Arenas', *Journal of Hispanic Research* 1 (1992), pp. 152–6.

Romney, Jonathan, 'Time to Strike Camp' [review of *Kika*], *New Statesman and Society* [London] (1 July 1994).

Root, Jane, review of *Improper Conduct*, *Monthly Film Bulletin*, vol. 52, no. 618 (1984), pp. 220–1.

Rouyer, Philippe, '*L'Ecureuil rouge*: double jeu' [review of *La ardilla roja*], *Positif* 398 (April 1994), pp. 52–3.

Rubio, Andrés F., 'Almodóvar ataca el sistema censor de EE UU en la presentación de *Kika* en Nueva York', *El País* (4 May 1994).

Sartori, Beatrice, '"Me interesa mucho seducir", dice Julio Medem: director revelación con *Vacas* ultima el rodaje de su segunda película, *La ardilla roja*', *El Mundo* (4 October 1992).

Sánchez Vidal, Agustín, *Sol y sombra* (Barcelona: Planeta, 1990).

Savater, Fernando, *Contra las patrias* (Barcelona: Tusquets, 1984).

Scheper-Hughes, Nancy and Robert Herrick, 'Ethical Tangles' [on AIDS in Cuba], *New Internationalist* (May 1992), p. 35.

Searle, Adrian, 'The Loss of Pepe Espaliú', in *Pepe Espaliú: Institute of Contemporary Arts, London, 4 March–17 April 1994* (London: ICA, 1994).

Smith, Paul Julian, 'Gianni Vattimo: Philosopher of Postmodernity', *Revista de Estudios Hispánicos* 25 (1991), pp. 109–16.

——, *Laws of Desire: Questions of Homosexuality in Spanish Writing and Film 1960–90* (Oxford: Oxford University Press, 1992).

——, *Desire Unlimited: The Cinema of Pedro Almodóvar* (London: Verso, 1994).

——, 'Future Chic' [on *Kika*], *Sight and Sound* (January 1994), pp. 6–10.

Sopeña Monsalve, Andrés, *El florido pensil: memoria de la escuela nacional-católica* (Barcelona: Crítica, 1994).

Strauss, Frédéric, 'The Almodóvar Picture Show', *Cahiers du Cinéma* 471 (September 1993), pp. 34–42.

——, *Pedro Almodovar* [sic]: *conversations avec Frédéric Strauss* (Paris: Cahiers du Cinéma, 1994).

Studlar, Gaylyn, *In the Realm of Pleasure: Von Sternberg, Dietrich, and the Masochistic Aesthetic* (New York: Columbia University Press, 1988).

Tesson, Charles, 'Docteur Fidel et Mister Raul' [review of *Mauvaise conduite*], *Cahiers du Cinéma* 358 (April 1984), pp. 47–8.

Teuber, Bernhard, 'Cuerpos sagrados: en torno a las imágenes perversas de la carne en España' (unpublished paper).

Torres, Augusto M., *Diccionario del cine español* (Madrid: Espasa Calpe, 1994).

Torres, Maruja, 'Pedro Almodóvar: "No me quiero morir nunca"', *El País* (25 September 1993), p. 22.

Trend, J. B., *Lorca and the Spanish Poetic Tradition* (Oxford: Basil Blackwell, 1956).

Turner, Ruth, and Lola Estrany, curators, *Members Only* [catalogue] (Barcelona: Galeria Carles Poy, 12 November – 20 December 1992).

Usieto Atondo, Ricardo, *Anomía y marginación social: poblaciones expuestas al SIDA* (Madrid: Complutense, 1992).

Vattimo, Gianni, *La fine della modernità* (Milan: Garzanti, 1985).

——, *La sociedad transparente*, trans. Teresa Oñate (Barcelona: Paidós, 1992).

Verdú, Vicente, ed., *Nuevos amores, nuevas familias* (Barcelona: Tusquets, 1992).

Vidal, Nuria, *El cine de Pedro Almodóvar* (Barcelona: Destino, 1988).

——, review of *Vacas*, *Fotogramas* (May 1992).

Vilarós, Teresa, 'Revuelo de plumas en la España de la transición', *Revista Cultural de Crítica* 8 (May 1994), pp. 20–5.

Virilio, Paul, *War and Cinema* (London: Verso, 1989).

——, *The Vision Machine* (London: BFI, 1994).

——, 'La vanguardia del olvido', *El País* (13 May 1994), pp. 13, 14.

Watney, Simon, 'The Subject of AIDS', in Peter Aggleton et al., eds, *AIDS: Social Representations, Social Practices* (New York: Falmer, 1989), pp. 64–73.

Weeks, Jeffrey, 'AIDS: The Intellectual Agenda', in Peter Aggleton et al., eds, *AIDS: Social Representations, Social Practices* (New York: Falmer, 1989), pp. 11–20.

Widdicombe, Rupert, 'Catalan Quota Sparks Backlash', *Screen International* (19 November 1993), p. 4.

Winston, Brian, *Claiming the Real: The Documentary Film Revisited* (London: BFI, 1995).

Wollen, Peter, *Raiding the Icebox: Reflections on Twentieth-Century Culture* (London: Verso, 1993).

INDEX

171

1629997

hell

DATE DUE

DEC 16 2008			
GAYLORD			PRINTED IN U.S.A.